STEVE McVEY

THE
SECRET
OF
GRACE

HARVEST HOUSE PUBLISHERS
EUGENE, OREGON

Cover by Left Coast Design, Portland, Oregon

Cover photo © Mr. Suwit Gaewsee-Ngam / Shutterstock

THE SECRET OF GRACE
Revised and updated edition of *Grace Rules*
Copyright © 1998, 2014 by Steve McVey
Published by Harvest House Publishers
Eugene, Oregon 97402
www.harvesthousepublishers.com

Library of Congress Cataloging-in-Publication Data
McVey, Steve, 1954-
 [Grace rules]
 The secret of grace / Steve McVey.
   pages cm
 ISBN 978-0-7369-5782-3 (pbk.)
 ISBN 978-0-7369-5783-0 (eBook)
 1. Salvation. 2. Grace (Theology) 3. Christian life. I. Title.
 BT751.3.M38 2014
 234—dc23
                                                                            2013015295

Printed in the United States of America

18 19 20 21 22 / BP-CD / 10 9 8 7 6 5 4 3 2

To Gabriel Steven McVey,
whose recent entrance into this
world is a gift to all of us.

Acknowledgments

Books are shaped within the context of the author's life. In other words, other people influence those who write the books. This is a great blessing to me because I have great people surrounding me, who constantly encourage me and fan the flame of grace in my own grace walk.

I am so thankful for the Grace Walk team I work beside in sharing this message. Each one of them has been such a gift to me as I've grown and moved forward in my own journey of grace. They are all exceptional teachers of grace who stand on the front line in spreading the message of our Father's unconditional love. I love every one of you.

I'm indebted to all the team at Harvest House Publishers. For almost two decades they have stood shoulder to shoulder with me in spreading the message of grace through the books I've written. I've not met one person there who doesn't express their role as a ministry first and business afterward. From the initial concept to the finished product, their fingerprints are on what I do. I'm particularly appreciative to Paul Gossard, my editor for this book. His insight and suggestions had an important part in causing this book to be what it is, and for that I'm grateful.

My endless thanks remain with Melanie, the love of my life. After 40 years of marriage, she is still the biggest influence on me in every good way. Who could have imagined the road we would travel? I am so glad I've traveled it with her.

Finally, and most importantly, I give any glory for anything good that may come from this book to my Savior. My very existence is in Him, and to Him I give praise for anything of real value that might flow from me.

Contents

Chapter 1

THE SECRET OF NOT TRYING

Opening His eyes, Jesus could see the early morning light beginning to filter in through the window of the small guest bedroom where He had spent the night. He could hear His friend already in the kitchen preparing breakfast. No doubt about it—the mother of all buffets was being prepared. Martha always put out a great spread of food. He loved being in the home of these two sisters and their brother. For a moment He wished He could take the day off and spend some time with them. *It would be nice*, He thought, *but the devil never takes a day off. And besides, My Father is counting on Me.*

Arising from the comfort of the bed, Jesus began to mentally organize His day. *What shall I do for My Father today?* He pondered. *I know that I'll preach a sermon this afternoon. That's one thing that will cause Father to really be happy with Me.* As He washed His face with a wet cloth, He continued, *There are many sick people in the area. I'll heal some of them. My Father would certainly be pleased with that. Maybe I'll even cast out some*

demons today. That's always a big ministry event. When He finished dressing, He thought, *Maybe if all goes well, I can even find
a funeral service and raise somebody from the dead. Yes. That's
what I'll do. Father will be thrilled when He sees Me take on a ministry project like that. Those things should pretty much fill My day.*
Slipping on His sandals just before walking out of the bedroom
to face the new day, He prayed, *Help Me, Father, as I try my best
to live for You today. Use what I do for You to bring glory to Yourself.*

A Reality Check

What are your thoughts on that scenario describing how
Jesus might have begun a new day? If it sounds pretty good to
you, I implore you, don't put down this book until you have finished reading it. I assume you know I have described this imaginary scene with tongue in cheek. Nobody would imagine Jesus
living His life in such a way. Jesus trying to score brownie points
with His Father? There's no way.

Yet for many years, I started my day in a similar way. I arose
each morning focusing on all the things I planned to do for God
during the day. I believed that the reason God opened my eyes
to Him was so I could serve Him, and I certainly tried my hard-
est to do that. I dedicated myself to living for Jesus.

I was diligent and sincere and often felt successful at it. With
my Bible in one hand and my Day-Timer in the other, I went
forward to make my mark for God in what I then saw as "this
heathen world."

I was a local church pastor for over 20 years and I was serious
about it. My life was dedicated to trying my best to serve Jesus
Christ. My behavior wasn't always consistent, but my desire was.
I wanted to live for Him and I tried my best to do the things I
thought He wanted me to do.

Even when I didn't think I was doing a good job of it, I still
wanted it. I believed everybody should try to do the things God
wants them to do and that, as a pastor, it was my calling to tell

them how to do it. Every week I would preach sermons intended to motivate the congregation to try harder, by God's help, to do the right things.

I did notice, however, that no matter how hard I tried, I always had an underlying sense I had failed to successfully accomplish my own internal to-do list that I carried every day of my life. When I felt like my efforts were successful I felt gratified, but I wouldn't have called it satisfying because I always felt a need to do more. I kept trying to live up to what I thought God wanted but I never felt like I had succeeded.

Twenty-nine years after I had first begun to trust Christ, He showed me something that shocked me. I'm going to let you in on this secret, but I must first warn you to brace yourself, because it goes against the conventional wisdom of the whole religious world, including the beliefs of many Christians.

In fact, if you didn't have any problem with the first few paragraphs of this chapter, you had better have a tongue depressor ready before you read the next statement, because you may need it.

God Doesn't Want Us to Try to Serve Him

God neither wants nor needs us to do anything for Him. What a blow to human pride! I had spent my lifetime trying to do the things I thought He wanted me to do! But now He was showing me that my whole paradigm had been wrong? That revelation shook my religious foundation into a pile of rubble.

I had always heard it said that we are the only hands that God has, we are the only feet He has, and we are His only eyes, ears, and mouth. As I think about it now, that's a scary thought. Jesus said that, if necessary, the rocks could cry out praise to Him. God once used a donkey to deliver a message to a prophet. While it's true that the Bible teaches we are the body of Christ, we find ourselves in a precarious position if we suggest that God's eternal agenda hinges on the success of our efforts as human beings.

When looking at modern Christianity, a person could conclude that God must be a quadriplegic if we were to say that the mobility of His agenda depends on our successful efforts in serving Him.

The Bible says in Acts 17:25, "Nor is He served by human hands, as though He needed anything, since He Himself gives to all people life and breath and all things." God simply doesn't need us. If you believe otherwise, I encourage you to take an honest inventory of all your abilities and assets and then compare those to the omnipotence of the God who stood on the vast edge of nothingness and said, "Let there be!" and there was. Stop reading and think about that for a moment. Now—what was it you have that God needs?

If you are troubled by the news that God doesn't need us, let me give you some news you will be glad to hear. The good news is that He *wants* us. He has set His love on us and has the desire to enjoy intimacy with us. I used to believe that the reason God wants us to know Him is so we can serve Him, but Jesus gave a different reason for God's giving us eternal life.

In a prayer to His Father, He said, "This is life eternal, that they might know thee the only true God, and Jesus Christ, whom Thou hast sent" (John 17:3 KJV). Jesus said that the reason we have been given eternal life is so that we may *know* Him and His Father intimately.

Ron and Mary Beth sat in my office, both totally exasperated. "I don't know what she wants," he said. "I try to do everything I can to make her happy and nothing satisfies her."

"Ron, I've told you the problem," she answered softly.

"She says that she doesn't feel I need and appreciate her," he went on. "She knows I need her. I couldn't run my business without her—and our home, well, that would be a mess without her," Ron answered, looking to me for understanding.

"That's just the problem," she answered. Turning to me she said, "I'm nothing more than an administrative assistant to him at work and a housekeeper at home. I don't have any doubt that he needs what I do, but he doesn't act like he needs *me*."

Mary Beth's problem illustrates well the misconception that many have about their relationship with God. They believe that their relationship with Him revolves around what they do for Him. They can't feel close to God because they think His primary interest is not in them, but in what they can do for Him. While Mary Beth may have been right about her husband, anybody who believes that her service to God is the basis of her relationship to Him is completely wrong. Our faith isn't about trying to serve Him effectively.

When we see our relationship to Him as being service-oriented, we will relate to Him as a divine Employer who scrutinizes our activity to make sure it is up to standard. Our focus will be on trying to improve our performance so we can successfully do the things we believe He requires.

This mindset reflects a legalistic view of what it means to be a Christian. It is a view that is completely erroneous. God doesn't want us to focus on trying to serve Him. The secret to living the life He wants us to know is to *stop trying* altogether. Our focus is to be Him, not our actions, looking through a self-judging lens to see how well we are or aren't doing.

Does this mean we are passive about activity? No, what it does mean is that we are to focus on Him with the confidence that our actions will be the natural overflow of the love relationship we have with Him. When we focus on trying to improve our performance, our whole "Christian lifestyle" becomes perfunctory and lifeless. When we are obsessed with Him, we don't have to try harder to do the right things. Our lifestyles literally become energized with divine life.

Jesus Never Tried to Do One Thing for God

I once read a church sign that declared, "Your life is God's gift to you. What you do with it is your gift to God." Nothing could be further from the teaching of the Bible. If we could make something out of our lives, there would be no need for Christ to have given Himself to us or have taken up residence in us. It really stokes our pride to think that we can do something for God. Yet the truth is that we cannot. Only God can do something for Himself. In His infinite grace, He allows us to participate in what He is doing by expressing His life through us.

The secret of not trying revolves around trusting Him as our life source instead of depending on our own determination and ability. If we aren't operating in the faith mode as opposed to the self-effort mode, then all we do adds up to zero. The key to living the overflowing life God intends for us to know is to trust, not try. We need to stop trying and simply trust.

How did Jesus live in this world? Didn't He try to do great things for His Father? No, He did not. Jesus came to reveal His Father to the world, but He didn't accomplish that goal by a lifestyle of trying out of His own strength and ability. Jesus once had a conversation with Philip that clearly shows how He functioned as a man in this world. John 14:8-10 records it:

> Philip said to Him, "Lord, show us the Father, and it is enough for us." Jesus said to him, "Have I been so long with you, and yet you have not come to know Me, Philip? He who has seen Me has seen the Father; how can you say, 'Show us the Father'? Do you not believe that I am in the Father, and the Father is in Me? The words that I say to you I do not speak on my own initiative, but the Father abiding in Me does His works."

Allow me to paraphrase and amplify that passage: Philip said to Jesus, "Lord, You sure talk a lot about Your Father. Why don't You just let us see Him and we will be satisfied?" Jesus answered him and said, "Philip, you don't have a clue, do you? Have I been with you this long and you still don't get it? If you have seen Me, you have seen the Father. Why are you asking Me to show you the Father? Don't you know that My Father and I are in total union together? Philip, the words that you hear Me speak aren't My words. My Father is speaking those words through Me. As for the things you see Me do, it's not Me doing those things. It is My Father, who is inside Me, who does those works."

Jesus very clearly stated that He was not the source of His own words and works. In John 14:24, He said about His speech, "The word which you hear is not Mine, but the Father's who sent Me." It was the Father—who is one with Jesus—who animated Jesus' life. He didn't try to do anything for His Father. The Father Himself did it through the union He shared with His Son.

For centuries theologians have debated what is called the "kenosis theory" in an attempt to explain the relationship between the humanity and deity of Jesus. The word *kenosis* comes from the Greek verb *kenoo*, which means "to empty or divest." When Jesus came into this world, He willingly emptied Himself of divine prerogatives. While retaining 100 percent of His deity, He chose not to live as God, but as a man who depended completely on God the Father. It is true that He was still God while He was here on earth, but He functioned totally as a man. He wanted to make it perfectly clear that He was a man just like us.

If the earthly life of Jesus can be described in terms of His Godhood, it offers us little encouragement. We could simply look at Jesus' lifestyle and say, "Well, of course He lived like that. After all, He is God!" Again, I emphasize that it is crucial to understand that the human lifestyle of Jesus can't be explained on the basis of His deity.

Let me put it another way: Do you know how many miracles Jesus could have done if it hadn't been His Father within Him doing the works? Not one. He couldn't have done a thing, no matter how hard He tried. Jesus could only do what God the Father was doing *through* Him. Don't take my word for it. Listen to what Jesus Himself had to say about it: "Truly, truly, I say to you, the Son can do nothing of Himself, unless it is something He sees the Father doing; for whatever the Father does, these things the Son also does in like manner" (John 5:19).

Jesus said that He could do nothing. Only as the Father expressed His powerful life through the Son did anything happen. Jesus didn't try to do one thing for God. Instead, He recognized the Father within Him, and God did everything Himself, through Jesus.

Jesus repeatedly asserted that His behavior didn't flow from His own self-efforts. He did nothing independent of His Father—*nothing*. Consider His own words in the following examples taken from the gospel of John:

> "I can do nothing on My own initiative" (John 5:30).

> "My teaching is not Mine, but His who sent Me" (John 7:16).

> "I do nothing on My own initiative, but I speak these things as the Father taught Me" (John 8:28).

> "I have not even come on My own initiative, but He sent Me" (John 8:42).

> "I did not speak on my own initiative, but the Father Himself who sent Me has given Me a commandment as to what to say and what to speak" (John 12:49).

Do you get the picture? Jesus lived as a normal man who was totally helpless apart from the divine enablement of His Father. He didn't *try* to do things for God but chose at every moment to live in total dependence on His heavenly Father.

Twenty-One Centuries Later

If the man Jesus found it necessary, not to depend on His own attempts at trying to live for God, but rather to depend on the Father to be expressed through Him, what makes us think that we can succeed in living the life God intends by *trying?* Before returning to His Father, Jesus made it clear to the disciples that they were to relate to Him in the same way He had related to the Father. In John 15, He used the metaphor of a vine and its branches to illustrate how believers were to live in the days to come. He said,

> "Abide in Me, and I in you. As the branch cannot bear fruit of itself, unless it abides in the vine, so neither can you, unless you abide in Me. I am the vine, you are the branches; he who abides in Me, and I in Him, he bears much fruit; for *apart from Me you can do nothing"* (verses 4-5).

The definitive issue in living as a follower of Christ today revolves around recognizing our dependence on Him. He asserts that there is nothing we can do *for* Him regardless of how hard we try. In the same way that the Father expressed His life through Jesus, we are to trust in Christ, allowing Him to express His life through us. We are simply to believe that our life is in Him, and depend on His life within us to cause us to be all that He has called us to be and to do all that he has purposed for us to do. Don't make this matter of abiding in Christ complicated; it simply means we recognize that we live in Him and He lives in us and then we choose to let Him do the living through us at every moment of our lives.

Jesus stated over and over again that nothing He did originated with Him. The source of His behavior was the life of the Father. He literally lived by the life of another Person. So it is to be in our lives today. Every action of our lives is to be animated by the life of the indwelling Christ. The key word is *trust,* not *try.*

The Word That Spoiled My Success in Living the Life He Intends

For 29 years one preposition spoiled my life. It kept me from enjoying my relationship with Christ and placed me under a constant strain. I thought it was my duty to live *for* Jesus. I don't want to get hung up on semantics here, but the emphasis of the New Testament is not on living *for* Christ, but on being *in* Christ. An understanding of what it means to be *in* Christ will totally transform a person's lifestyle.

In my book *Grace Walk*, I describe in detail my own pilgrimage from a lifetime of legalistic trying to the place where I began to experience legitimate trusting in Christ and His ability to cause my behavior to be what He wants without my huffing and puffing to get it right by my own determination. The words *for* Christ and *in* Christ may represent two totally different systems of living. *Trying* is one of them. It is a life of legalism. *Trusting*—the life of grace—is the other.

For much of my life my idea of living *for* Jesus meant dedicating myself to doing the things He would want me to do. I read the Bible primarily to discover principles for living a godly lifestyle. I regularly committed myself to those principles. I sometimes told people that I lived by my convictions. It was my belief that if a person committed himself to obeying the Scriptures, God would bless him. That, however, is the perfect description of a legalistic lifestyle. It is an attempt to gain God's blessings and to make spiritual progress based on what we do. It is a description of a lifestyle burdened down by legalistic effort instead of lifted up by grace-filled energy.

There was a major problem I faced every time I seriously examined the Bible to see if I was measuring up to what I thought God expected of me. I always discovered other commands I wasn't yet fully obeying. Consequently, I never felt completely satisfied, because I always saw how far I still had to go before I would reach the place I thought I needed to be spiritually. I was committed to biblical principles and I sincerely wanted to live for Jesus. Those may sound like noble aspirations, yet in reality they are subtle deceptions. Christianity is not about doing things *for* Christ. It is about being *in* Him. Ironically, it is when we live from that truth that we find our lifestyles conforming to what the Bible says about godly living.

Compliance Without Obedience

Authentic Christianity is not a call to live by principles or to try our best to live for Jesus. To build our lives around biblical principles sounds admirable, but it is a subtle form of legalism. Of course there are teachings in the New Testament about how we are to live. Yet these instructions are not religious challenges we are to try to follow. They are descriptions of the many ways Christ can live His life though us as we depend on Him. New Testament Christianity is not grounded in what we do, but in what He has already done.

The Bible teaches that the One who has begun the work in us will also be the One who completes it. Paul said, "Faithful is He who calls you, *and He will also bring it to pass*" (1 Thessalonians 5:24). The Bible is clear: Jesus will do it, not us.

There is indeed a blessing to be enjoyed as we obey the Lord, but simply doing what God says does not produce blessings. Sitting at my computer one day, I opened my e-mail to find a note from my friend Roger. "Steve, why can't I find this great life the Bible talks about?" he asked. "As far as I know, I'm doing everything God says to do. I've given up the sins of my past, but I feel like I'm still wandering around in circles. Help me find the answer!"

Can you see where Roger's problem was? He states the exact reason why he believed he should be enjoying an abundant life. "I'm doing everything God says to do. I've given up the sins of my past." Roger was experiencing the results of *compliance*, not obedience. Simply doing what God says has never brought joy to anybody's life. The source of joy is Jesus Himself, not mere compliance with the Bible's commands.

Many people struggle with the question, "Why am I not fulfilled when I'm trying my best to do all the things I believe

God wants me to do?" It's because they haven't discovered the secret of not trying. God's purpose is not that we should focus on doing the right things. Rather, He wants us to focus on Him. *Obedience happens when we trust Jesus within us to fulfill the desires of His Father through us.* As He does that, we will fulfill the commands of the Scriptures. On the other hand, when we simply do what the Bible instructs, that is not godly obedience. It is nothing more than *compliance.*

Sometimes we can comply with Bible commands in the same way that anybody can choose at any given moment to make the right choice instead of the wrong one. For instance, the Bible says not to steal. The fact is that anybody can live up to that standard, whether they are following Christ or not. However, just making the right choice is not obedience. That kind of choice is nothing more than empty compliance. Trying can accomplish that much. It takes no trust in Christ at all.

Why Can't We Live the Christian Life?

What has commonly been called "the Christian life" is typically more cultural than Christ-centered. It is often a cheap counterfeit marked by trying to behave based on a biblical template instead of living in simple trust in Christ. Authentic Christian living is nothing less than an expression of divine life though mortal man. Many people struggle because they fail to understand God's method, by which they may experience consistent success in living the life He designed for them. Why can't they live that lifestyle? The bottom line is this: God never intended for them to live it. Only one Person has ever been able to live the Christ-life. That Person is Christ Jesus Himself.

All believers understand they did nothing to become Christians. They simply trusted Christ. Yet many believe they must now try hard to do the right things to become a good Christian. So for faith, they substitute a fight to do right. Then they wonder why it won't work. The fact is, it will never work. It's not supposed to work! No matter how sincere they may be, how hard they may try, or how much they may ask for God's help, they will never be able to live the life God wants them to enjoy. It isn't hard for them to live it; it's impossible! If you haven't seen that yet, give it time and you will. However, I assume you may already suspect that to be the case.

For many years, I didn't know how to experience consistency in my spiritual journey because I didn't understand the whole story of salvation. I knew enough to believe I was going to heaven but not enough to enjoy heaven on earth. I understood mercy but not grace.

Meet Mercy and Grace

The power of the finished work of Jesus on the cross has permanently dealt with the issue of sin's penalty. As our substitute there, He took all our sin off us and onto Himself. When He said, "It is finished," those words gave complete assurance that the sin issue in your life has been forever settled. Sin exacts a penalty. It demands that a debt be paid. "The wages of sin is death," the apostle Paul wrote in Romans 3:23. Just as surely as poor eating and exercise habits bring the penalty of health problems, sin brings the penalty of death. It was that penalty that Jesus took on our behalf. It wasn't the Father who punished Jesus, but sin itself that brought that horrible penalty of death upon our Lord. (Our heavenly Father and the Holy Spirit were equally involved in our salvation. See 2 Corinthians 5:19 and Hebrews 9:14) Thankfully, through faith in Him we are now able to be forever free from the wages of sin.

In His wondrous mercy, our great God has taken it all upon and into Himself. Jesus never sinned, but He took our sin as His own and, consequently, paid the price by sacrificing Himself in our place. He didn't deserve to pay the price for sin although we did. His death is an expression of His mercy toward us.

Many years ago when I served as a local pastor in an Alabama church, I was driving from Birmingham back to my church about an hour away. When I exited the interstate I didn't adjust my speed for the highway I entered. In a few moments I heard a siren and saw the flashing blue lights in my rearview mirror. Glancing down at my speedometer, I thought, *Oh, no! Now I've done it. I'm caught.*

The policeman walked up to my window and asked to see my driver's license. "Sir, do you know how fast you were going?" he asked.

"Yes, sir, I do," I answered, trying to look as "reverendly" as I knew how.

"Would you please step out of the car and sit in the front seat of the squad car?" he asked in a matter-of-fact way.

I quickly walked back to his car and sat down in the front seat, cowering and hoping that none of my church members would drive by and see their pastor in the front seat of a police car. After showing me my recorded speed on his radar, the policeman reached for his ticket book. He opened it and took his pen out of his pocket. Just as he flipped to the right place, I said, "Officer?"

"Yes?" he responded.

"Will you give me mercy?" I asked. The policeman looked at me for a moment, looked down at his ticket book, and then looked back at me.

"Okay, I'll do it," he answered. "Slow down, and have a safe day."

That really happened! (Don't think that's how it always is with preachers. Another policeman who gave me a ticket said that of all people I should know better than to break the law.) Do you see what happened? I deserved the ticket, but the officer gave me a break. I didn't get what I deserved.

That's how the mercy of God is expressed toward us. We all deserve to pay the full penalty for sin. If we look at it on the basis of *deserving*, nothing else is even logical (see Romans 3:23). It would certainly be fair that we be the ones to pay the price called for by sin. After all, we are the ones who sinned. Yet, knowing what sin would do to us and in advance of sin even rearing its ugly head in this world, our God chose to extend His mercy toward us by coming into this world and handling the matter Himself. He didn't do anything wrong—we did. However, the triune love of the Father, Son, and Holy Spirit compelled Him to act on our behalf by rescuing us from sin's penalty, taking it into Himself. That's mercy!

Yet there is another aspect of the gospel that many people don't understand. Let's go back to that policeman in Alabama. Some people said to me, "That guy really showed you grace, didn't he?" The answer to that question is no. He showed me no grace whatsoever, only mercy.

However, suppose that before I drove away from him, the policeman had said to me, "Wait just a minute. I'm not finished with you yet." Imagine if he then reaches into his pocket, pulls out his wallet, and hands me a $100 bill. "I want you to have this," he says. "Have a great day." Now *that* would have been grace! (Sadly, that part of the story didn't happen.)

Mercy happens when we don't receive something we deserve, and grace is receiving something we don't deserve. God showed us mercy when He took our place, taking the punishment due from sin upon Himself even though we were the ones who had sinned. Then He went a step further and extended His grace to us, giving us divine life by taking up residence in us in the Person of His Spirit. Mercy is wonderful, but it wasn't the main thing in salvation's story. The main thing is that Christ has brought us into Himself, thus freeing us from having to try to live for God. We can simply trust Him for our salvation both in eternity and in our daily lifestyle. The secret of not trying is wonderful because we don't *need* to try. He has done it all on our behalf and will now live it out through us each day.

Why Does Jesus Live Inside Us?

Have you ever stopped to consider why Jesus has chosen to take up residence in you? He promised His disciples that after He left this earth physically, His Spirit would come and live inside them (see John 14:16-17). Why does the Spirit of Jesus live inside us? Consider some of the misunderstandings about the answer to that question:

1. *Jesus came into us so our sins can be forgiven.* It's not necessary for Jesus to live inside you for your sins to be forgiven. Could God have forgiven us without placing His life inside us? Yes, His mercy would have taken care of that without the grace of having Christ indwell us.

2. *He came into us so we can go to heaven.* Does Jesus live inside us so we can go to heaven when we die? Why would it be necessary for Him to live in us on this earth just for that reason? He could take us to heaven without placing His life within us.

3. *Jesus lives inside us so we will know how to live.* Is He inside us so we can know what to do in life? No, because if the issue revolved around living a particular way, the Bible gives us enough information to know it. We don't need Jesus living in us for that reason.

There is one simple reason why the Spirit of Jesus Christ lives inside you. It is so you can experience life in the Godhead and express His divine life. Jesus clearly said that He came so we might have *life* (see John 10:10). In Him, we have been made alive (see Ephesians 2:1-7). The fundamental characteristic of your life is that Jesus has given His life to you and desires to express it through you at every moment.

The secret to a life of grace has nothing to do with *me* trying to serve Jesus. It's not *me* living for Him. It's not *me* trying to do the things I think God is instructing me to do. A life in grace is *Him*! This grace walk is nothing less than the Christ-life. It is New Testament Christianity, not the hybrid version that has so polluted authentic Christianity by insisting we must try to do things for Him. The pure faith of the early New Testament church is nothing less and nothing more than Christ *being* Christ in us and through us at every moment.

For 29 years of my journey in faith, I diligently tried to live for Jesus. Although I truly knew Him, law (religious rules) governed my life. What a wonderful discovery it was when I realized I couldn't live for Him and didn't need to try to live for Him. In fact, my trying to live for Him actually interfered with His purposes.

God doesn't need us to live for Him. He will live through us as we live in absolute dependence on Him at each moment. This is exactly what it means to embrace "the secret of not trying."

WALKING TOGETHER

Let's walk together with the Holy Spirit through this book. As God reveals truth to you, it will be helpful to participate with Him at each step where He works in your life. If the prayers at the end of each chapter express your heart, then affirm to God that they reflect your thoughts and desires. You will get more out of this book if you pause at the end of each chapter and interact with your heavenly Father.

Dear Father,

I have experienced a struggle in my life as I've tried to live for You. I see that at times I've focused more on my own behavior than I have on Jesus. I now understand that I'm not supposed to try to live for You, but instead I am to allow You to live Your life though me. Teach me how to experience obedience motivated by love instead of duty. I can't live the life You have designed for me in my own power. Show me how You can live Your life through me. Right now, I give up my futile attempts at trying to live the right way. Instead, I trust You to live Your life through me in my daily lifestyle.

❦ GROUP QUESTIONS

At the end of each chapter you will find discussion questions to help facilitate further learning and discussion. The truths of this book will be worked further into your life as you consider these questions.

1. Read Acts 17:25. What is your opinion of the idea that God doesn't need us to serve Him? What difference will it make in a person's perspective if he believes that God *needs* him as opposed to the idea that God *wants* him?

2. The "kenosis theory" suggests that Jesus emptied Himself of divine prerogatives. Explain the importance of the theory in view of John 5:19. What difference would it make if the lifestyle of Jesus had been sustained by His divine nature?

3. List five differences between living *for* Christ and living *in* Christ.

4. What is the difference between compliance and obedience?

5. Define *mercy* and *grace*. What is the difference between the two? What is the result of experiencing God's mercy? What is the result of experiencing His grace?

6. Read John 14:16-17. Why does the Spirit of Jesus (the Holy Spirit) live in you? How can trying to live for Jesus out of our own strength cause problems in life?

7. Describe "the secret of not trying." Why is this secret so important in living the life God intends for us to know and enjoy?

Chapter 2

THE SECRET OF WEAKNESS

The man felt a surge of anger at the sight of his brother being mercilessly beaten by a brutal bully. This one he loved lay crumpled in the dirt with his hands over his head, trying to protect himself from the attack. Having beaten him to the ground, the attacker now kicked him in the side as his victim groaned in agony. The man instinctively moved forward toward the attacker and his victim. Looking around as he advanced, he saw that there was no one else in sight. Just this evil bully, his helpless victim, and himself.

Coming up from behind, he struck the assailant hard on the back of his head. Very hard. The bully staggered backward, trying to keep his balance. The man drew back and with all his strength struck him again. The assailant fell to the ground. He didn't make a sound. He wasn't breathing. Blood began to ooze out of his nose and ears. It was obvious—he was dead.

The victim stared at his attacker for a moment, then looked up at his rescuer. He didn't say a word, but quickly turned and ran. In spite of his injuries, he ran fast. The man watched him disappear into a nearby building, then looked around again. He still saw no one. Hurriedly he pulled the corpse up from the ground and dragged it away. He must dispose of the body before anyone knew what he had done. He felt justified in what had happened, but the authorities wouldn't understand. He must hide the body quickly before he was discovered.

Only one person had seen what he did. Just one. Yet because of that one man, he was to become a fugitive from the law. For 40 years he would go into hiding.

A PG-Rated Story in a G-Rated Book

Does this story sound like a movie preview you have seen? It's a story about espionage and murder and a fleeing felon. However, the scene didn't come from a movie script. It came from a book. It is found in the Bible in Exodus chapter 2. The main character who becomes a fugitive is Moses. He is mentioned in Hebrews 11 as a man of great faith, but he didn't start out that way. We are told in Exodus 2:11 that Moses had grown up, and then in the very next verse we are told he became a murderer. Not exactly the way you would expect the story of a man's adult life to begin, a man who would ultimately become one of the greatest servants of God who ever lived.

Among the men of the Bible whose lives had major impact on this world, none offer more hope for the average man than Moses. Although he lived millennia before the cross, his life reflects the grace-filled manner in which God prepares those whom He intends to use for His own glory. Unless you have murdered somebody, you're already one step ahead of Moses in the journey toward a fulfilling and distinguished life. Even if you have murdered somebody, you're no further from God's plan than he was at the beginning of his adulthood.

Josh came to me one day, obviously discouraged. "Steve, I don't know what my problem is. Maybe I've done too many wrong things for God to ever be able to use me. I can't seem to experience a life that seems worth living. I guess I'm just a weak person." I knew his background. He had made some serious mistakes in judgment, even after he had begun to follow Christ. Now he was convinced that his sins disqualified him from being useful to God.

Have you ever felt like that? When we try to understand why we aren't experiencing fulfillment in life, we often tend to look in the wrong place to find answers. Josh believed that it was his moral weakness that prevented him from finding what he was looking for in life. Yet his weakness wasn't the problem at all. If God only used sinless people, every one of us would be disqualified.

Moses saw himself as strong. Josh saw himself as weak. Moses started out depending on personal strength, and Josh thought he needed more of it. Both were wrong.

There's a secret that you need to know about weakness. It's a good thing. That's right, a *good* thing. Society's messages have always told us we need to become strong. "If it's going to be, it's up to me," we've been taught. "If at first you don't succeed, try, try again," has become the mantra of many do-it-yourselfers. The fact is, despite all the messages to the contrary, this is simply the wrong approach in God's kingdom.

Many people think we need to be strong if we are going to honor God with our lives. The reality is that we don't become strong enough for Him to work in our lives. The life He intends for us to know has nothing to with *our* strength. Instead, we have to become weak enough. We may dedicate our abilities to God, asking Him to help us to use them for His glory. While that sounds admirable, it is actually the surest way to experience continual defeat. Josh had to discover that he wasn't too weak to be used by God. It wasn't more personal strength he needed. In fact, he was already too strong. His motive was right but, like Moses in the beginning, his method for living was totally wrong.

The Right Motive and the Wrong Method

Moses certainly was motivated by a right desire. All of his life he had inwardly identified with his own people. Seeing an Egyptian taskmaster beating his Jewish brother deeply stirred his compassion. Moses sensed deep within himself a desire to free the people of Israel. It was within his very nature to want to deliver the Jews from Egyptian oppression. God had put that life calling into him. He saw a need and wanted to do something about it. A God-given desire motivated him. However, he made one fatal mistake—he thought he was strong enough to get the job done.

Depending on his own personal strength, he moved forward to do what he believed would be the right thing. In time, he would discover that trying to do something right, even something God intended for him to do, out of his own strength would ultimately lead to major defeat.

The fact that you're reading a book like this one is a fairly good indicator that you have a sincere interest in spiritual matters. You most likely want to live in a way that would fit God's plan for your life. Many of us feel that way. The breakdown comes when we possess the same faulty viewpoint Moses had—thinking we must be strong in order to live the life we are intended to live.

For almost three decades of my spiritual journey, I fell into this trap. I sensed an inner desire to live a life that honored God. I sincerely wanted my life to make a difference in this world. So I dedicated myself to Him and tried to use my abilities for His glory. As with Moses, my motive was right. However, my method was wrong. God never asks us to use our ability to do anything for Him. His plan is that we rely totally on His ability, not ours. It is not by our might or power that His work is accomplished, but rather it's by the strength of His Spirit within us. Many Christians live in defeat and frustration because they can't experience the spiritual life they want in spite of all their right desires and good intentions. Their problem lies in believing they need to be strong. An amazing aspect of this matter is that God doesn't want strong people but weak people. That way it is obvious He is the One who achieved what was accomplished.

The prescribed method for our lifestyle is clearly set forth in the book of Acts when Peter preached on the day of Pentecost. In speaking of the lifestyle of Jesus in this world, Peter plainly tells how He lived:

> Men of Israel, listen to these words: Jesus the Nazarene, a man attested to you by God with miracles and wonders and signs which *God performed through Him* in your midst…(Acts 2:22).

The Bible says that it was God who performed the miracles, wonders, and signs through Jesus. Our Lord did not live out of His own human strength. He lived from out of the infinite strength of His Father. Peter stresses the fact that Jesus was a man who relied on His Father to accomplish His work. If Jesus chose to depend totally on His Father to animate and empower His lifestyle, what makes us think we can do anything for God through our own natural abilities?

The Seminary of Suffering

Moses possessed such an overpowering desire to free his people. His determination was so extreme that it appeared he was going to deliver these Jews if he had to do it by taking out one Egyptian at a time! He may have reasoned that he might not be strong enough to bring them all down at once, but he could certainly do his best one by one. He still had much to learn about God's methods. He didn't know it, but the Lord was making plans for him to enroll in seminary so he could learn His way of doing things.

The day after Moses killed the Egyptian, he went out and saw two Hebrews fighting with each other. He rushed up to them and asked, "Why are you hitting your friend?" One of the men asked him, "Who made you an authority to judge us? Are you intending to kill me like you did the Egyptian?"

Moses' blood ran cold. He knew he was caught. Just as he feared, Pharaoh heard about the incident and tried to kill him. So Moses ran, narrowly escaping into the desert of Midian. He hardly suspected that God was there ahead of him, waiting in the desert to teach him a truth that would totally transform his life. It's the same truth that can change your life.

How quickly circumstances can change. One day Moses was living in the courts of Pharaoh. The next day he is living in the desert. He no longer smells the fragrant perfume of royal beauties, but instead the stench of unwashed sheep fills his nostrils. No linen sheets cover his bed tonight. He sleeps on a bed of straw under the stars. He has exchanged the robes of royalty for the tattered tunic of a shepherd. Everything is gone. It's all lost. He was a prince, but now he is a lowly shepherd. All that power...vanished. Why would God allow this to happen to a man whose only desire was to deliver a godly people from wicked oppressors?

In 1989 I felt I was a successful pastor. I was serving a growing church. I received constant affirmation and recognition. In all the ways that I measured success back then, I felt validated and good about myself. Then God took me to a place where all that changed. All the things that had worked for me in the past didn't work anymore. In fact, nothing I did worked. I blamed myself. I blamed my church. I even blamed God. Over a period of time, He began to teach me the secret that He took Moses to the wilderness to learn—the secret of weakness.

God doesn't want us to depend on the strength we can muster through self-will and determination. That's how those who don't know better try to get things done, but it doesn't work that way in the kingdom of God. Like Moses, many of us must discover this the hard way. We usually learn it living in a dry and barren place.

Don't believe the lie that God has forgotten you when you find yourself living in difficult circumstances. He has a reason for your being there. Stop blaming Satan for it too. Don't give the devil the glory for your troubles! God is sovereign over the enemy, and He will use your pain to accomplish His purposes. God will use the desert experiences of life to shake away from us everything except Him. The lie may flood your mind that God doesn't care about what is happening to you, but He does! He loves us so much that He will even work through our pain to bring us into a dependent relationship with Him.

When my son David was about three years old, he woke up one night crying in agony. My wife Melanie and I rushed into his bedroom and could immediately tell something was seriously wrong. We agreed she would stay at home with the other children and I would take him to the hospital. When we arrived at the emergency room, the attending physician examined him. He turned to me and said, "I know your son's problem. David has an intestinal blockage that must be cleared. Neither his bladder nor bowels have emptied in a long time. That's the reason he's experiencing intense pain."

"What has to be done?" I asked.

"Two things," the doctor answered. "First, it will be necessary to catheterize him." I shuddered at the thought. "Then, we must also administer a barium enema," the doctor continued.

After he assured me that there were no other treatment options, I laid David down on the examining table. When the doctor began the procedure with the catheter, David started to come up off the table. "You'll have to hold him down," the doctor instructed me. Leaning across the body of my three-year-old son, I placed my right arm over his left shoulder and my left arm over his right shoulder so he couldn't move. David began to cry, hysterically screaming, "Daddy, make him stop! Daddy, please! Make him stop! Make him stop!" Then there was that moment—sort of like suspended animation—one of those frozen-in-time moments you never forget as long as you live. David stopped crying, looked deeply into my eyes, and with obvious terror and confusion asked, "Daddy, *why* won't you make him stop?"

How do you explain a catheter to a three-year-old? How could his young mind understand a valid reason for such pain? I couldn't answer because he couldn't understand even if I did. I began to cry too. I laid myself down across him and hugged him close to me and to the table. "It's okay, son. Daddy's here with you. You must trust me, David. This is necessary. It's for your good. I'll hold you until it's over."

I can remember times in my own life when I have cried out to my heavenly Father, "Make it stop! Make it stop! *Why* won't you make it stop?" Have you been there? Maybe you are at that place in life right now. Circumstances may not make sense. It may seem that God has abandoned you, but He hasn't. He may be holding you on the table so you can't get up, but *He is hugging you*! Jesus has joined you in the darkness. He takes no pleasure in your pain, yet He loves you enough that if it takes pain to bring you to the place where He can accomplish His purpose for your good, He will allow it as long as necessary. Be assured He won't keep you on the table a minute longer than necessary.

The Poison of Confidence in Self

God had plans for Moses in the wilderness. The first 40 years of his life had been majestic. The last 40 years would be miraculous, as he led the people out of Egypt and through the desert. However, these middle 40 years were miserable, not because God was making Moses miserable but because it took that long for him to let go of his self-sufficiency. That kind of stubbornness is often the gateway to misery, but our Father's love is always bigger than our stubbornness. God was bringing Moses to the end of himself and confidence in *his* own strength, so he might know and rest in the strength of God.

Moses had exchanged his identity from that of a prince to one of a shepherd. He probably saw himself as a survivor. Being a shepherd wasn't exactly the way he had thought things would turn out, but he was making the best of a bad situation. At least he had ability as a shepherd. Then came the burning bush.

In Exodus 3–4, the account of Moses' encounter with God is told. God reveals to him that He plans to use him to deliver the people from bondage. By this time, Moses has developed some serious doubts about his ability as a leader. He fears that having only lived with animals all these years, he may have lost his people skills. He may have reasoned, "The only ability I can count on anymore is my skill as a shepherd." Then God speaks:

> "What is that in your hand?" And he said, "A staff." Then He said, "Throw it on the ground." So he threw it on the ground, and it became a serpent; and Moses fled from it (Exodus 4:2-3).

Have you ever felt like God has taken everything He can take, and then it seems like He finds something else to take away from you? That's where Moses was in this passage. The staff was a symbol of Moses' ability as a shepherd. It wasn't much, but at least he was surviving through his ability to herd sheep.

Then God says about the staff, representing the ability in which he was still trusting, "Throw it down." When Moses threw the staff to the ground, it became a serpent. Finally he saw what God wanted him to see. He still had not come to the end of himself. He may have thought that though he wasn't a strong national leader, he possessed the strength to be a great shepherd.

He had simply exchanged his abilities as a prince for his abilities as a shepherd. Both types of strengths were simply two different ways of managing his life. Now he saw this for what it was. The very self-confidence and personal strength he had been trusting in had been poisonous to him all along and he hadn't even known it!

Mike began to talk to me one day about his frustration. "Steve, I don't get it. Before I began to walk with Christ, I partied. I drank too much, made immoral choices, and even experimented with drugs. When I became a Christian I turned my back on all that. I'm involved in my church now. I teach a boys' Sunday-school class. I sing in the choir. I try to be available to the pastor anytime he needs someone to do something."

As we talked further, I finally suggested what I believed his problem to be. "Mike, it sounds to me like you used to try to get your need for fulfillment met in the wrong ways."

"I did," he answered.

"Have you ever considered that you might still be trying to find fulfillment in the wrong way?" I asked. Mike look puzzled, so I continued: "It seems that maybe you've simply traded a bad identity for a better identity. You don't see yourself as a party animal anymore. Now you see yourself as a church worker."

"So what's wrong with working in the church?" he asked.

"Nothing is wrong with it. It can be a good thing, but God didn't plan for us to find fulfillment in good things. He desires that we be fulfilled in Him." As we continued to talk, Mike began to see the problem. Although he wasn't relying on his old identity to get his needs met, he was still relying on what *he* could do.

Moses had exchanged a royal life for a shepherd's life but had not yet experienced God's Life! He was thinking that the only ability he could count on anymore was his strength as a shepherd—but God was showing him that he couldn't even depend on that. We can only experience the Life of God when we throw down our lives. Jesus said in Matthew 16:25, "Whoever wishes to save his life will lose it; but whoever loses his life for My sake will find it." We only experience God's Life when we renounce dependence on our personal strength to succeed in life.

Harvey sat down across from me. "I don't understand my

life, Steve. I am a successful businessman. I have a good marriage. My kids are well behaved. Our finances are secure. Yet I can't seem to live the life I know God wants me to live. Why can I succeed in so many areas and still be an utter failure in the most important area of my life?"

"Do you want my honest opinion?" I asked him.

"Of course," he answered.

"Harvey, I think you're too polished for your own good. You've achieved success in the other major areas of your life and people admire you for it. You are an achiever, there's no doubt about it."

"Then what's the problem?" he interrupted.

"The problem is that you can't *achieve* victory in your grace walk. You can only *receive* it."

Harvey made a mistake that is common. A spiritually successful life isn't the result of strong determination on our part, but instead comes from divine strength being channeled through us. We must renounce confidence in our own personal strength, acknowledging that it is only by His indwelling life we can accomplish anything of value. There is nothing wrong with natural ability. It is God who has given us the abilities we possess. However, we must recognize the inherent danger that comes with ability. *Personal strength becomes a barrier in our grace walk when we trust in what we think we can accomplish instead of trusting in God.*

Moses looked at the serpent representing his ability and saw that fact. He was repulsed by how he had trusted in his own strength at all. He wanted nothing to do with it ever again. The Bible says that he "fled from it." Yet it wasn't the ability itself that was wrong; it was his sense of self-sufficiency that he attached to his ability. He never wanted to live that way again.

Strength That Comes from God

Having seen the folly of trusting in his own strength, it is now safe for Moses to take his abilities back up. God tells him to "'stretch out your hand and grasp it by its tail'—so he stretched out his hand and caught it, and it became a staff in his hand" (Exodus 4:4). Picking up the serpent by the tail certainly would have made Moses very aware of his vulnerability toward what he held in his hand. The only way he could ensure he wouldn't be infected with its venom was if he continually trusted the Lord to protect him from it. None of us ever reach the place where we become immune to the venom of the confidence in ourselves instead of Christ. The staff we hold always has the potential of becoming a poisonous serpent in our hands. We must trust in Christ moment by moment, realizing that without His empowering presence a self-sufficient dependence on ourselves will strike us, infecting us with its poison.

Once we have seen the error of placing confidence in what we think we can do, we are in a place where we have learned the secret of weakness. We know it's okay for us to be weak because it's not our own strength we're going to rely on. It is then that we can be trusted with the abilities God has given us. We will then be allowed to pick them back up, depending on Him to animate that same ability by His strength. Before, our abilities were empowered by self-determination; now the very Life of Jesus Christ animates them.

When God first asked Moses what he held in his hand, he answered, "A staff." However, in Exodus 4:20, when Moses is preparing to leave the desert and go back to Egypt where he will fulfill his calling, the Bible says, "Moses also took the staff of God in his hand." From that point forward in Scripture it would never be called "a staff," but would always be known as "the staff of God." Once God has brought us to the end of self-confidence, although others may not see the change that has taken place in our attitude toward natural ability, we know. To others it's the same old stick, but within our heart we know that our natural strength has been transformed into supernatural strength that we possess by virtue of His Life within us.

When Miracles Happen

When God brought me to the end of myself in 1990, He caused me to be repulsed by how much I had tried to become stronger. When I saw it, like Moses, I wanted to run. When the day came that I began to learn about trusting in His supernatural strength and not my own, the difference was like night and day. I'll never forget the first time I saw what God could do if I would trust Him instead of myself.

Philippe knocked on the door of my office one day. He introduced himself to me and we began to discuss why he was in Atlanta. I discovered that his home was Cameroon and that he had come to Georgia to study hospital administration. As we talked, it became apparent that Philippe was not a follower of Jesus. During that first visit together I was able to share the gospel with him, and he believed the good news of Jesus Christ. We agreed that he would come back each Tuesday morning and I would teach him from the Bible how to live the new life he had just come to know.

Every week he came to my office, and for two hours I shared with him from Scripture concerning what it means to be a Christian. We talked about who he was in Christ and about what it means to trust in Jesus moment-by-moment. We studied how to allow Jesus to live His life through us. I was happy to see the spiritual growth he was experiencing as he became more grounded in Christ.

After about six weeks he paused before leaving at the end of our time together. "Steve, have you noticed that I always take notes when we study together?" he asked.

"Yes, I have," I answered.

"Do you know why I take extensive notes while you are teaching me?" he continued.

"Well, I assume that you take them back to your apartment and study them during the following week," I answered.

"No, that's not it," he said. "You see, each week I write

everything you say on paper in my native language. Then when I leave here, I place the notes into a package and immediately go to the post office, where I mail the package to the chief of my village at home. Every week when he receives the notes, he goes outside and calls the people of my village together. Then he teaches them from the notes all the things you have taught me. Some of the people of my village are coming to faith in Christ and are asking the chief questions about this life in Him. He doesn't know the answers, so he writes and asks me, but I don't know the answers either. I told him I would ask you if you would be willing to answer their questions if I translate for you."

Suddenly it hit me. I thought of all the years I had tried to produce something spiritual…all the time I had spent trying to make a difference. I had sincerely used my abilities for God. I had applied every ounce of my strength to serving Him but had always felt frustrated. Now here was God doing it Himself. I was sitting in Atlanta, Georgia, with one black man sitting across my desk from me, and I was evangelizing and discipling a whole village of people in Africa. Only God can do that!

A miracle is an act of God that defies human understanding. Do you know when miracles happen? We will see the miraculous work of God in and through us to the extent that we renounce self-sufficient expressions of strength and rest in the all-sufficient Holy Spirit within us.

When Moses left the desert, having recognized the foolishness of trusting in his own strength, he returned to Egypt expecting miracles as the norm of life. God told him that he would "perform before Pharaoh all the wonders which I have put in your power." A man who has been broken of confidence in himself, yet who has absolute confidence in God, is one who can be entrusted with power to perform wonders.

When Peter and John met the lame man at the gate of the temple in Jerusalem, Peter took the man's hand and told him to get up and walk. The man, who had been lame from the day of his birth, began to walk, then run, and finally leap for joy. The crowd pressed in around Peter, amazed by his ability to perform such a feat. They thought he had impressive spiritual strength. Yet Peter knew the truth. He had learned about his own strength on the night he failed to stand for Jesus after promising that he would die for him if necessary. He quickly answered the crowd, "Why are you amazed at this, or why do you gaze at us, *as if by our own power* or piety we had made him to walk?" (Acts 3:12). He then immediately pointed them to Jesus as the cause of what they had witnessed.

Peter had learned the value of the strength of Christ functioning through him. So did Moses. Why would anybody today settle for what human strength can accomplish when we have the opportunity to experience the supernatural results of God's strength? He has prepared something great for every one of us. Willingness to renounce confidence in our own strength and embrace the secret of weakness is a vital step of preparation for receiving the recipe for experiencing the outflow of God's divine Life.

 ## Walking Together

Dear Father,

I see it now. The problem hasn't been that I haven't had the desire to glorify You. I've been going about trying to live the wrong way. All this time that I've been trying to live for You, I have thought that my need was to be stronger. Now I see that this isn't the need and it will never work. Right now I willingly lay down my strength. My confidence in it has poisoned my life. I never want to trust in my strength again. I trust only You, Lord Jesus. Teach me how to experience Your strength flowing through me.

GROUP QUESTIONS

1. Read Exodus 2:11-15. How did Moses initially depend on his own strength to deliver Israel from Egyptian bondage? Discuss ways that modern congregations sometimes depend on natural ability to facilitate church ministry.

2. What would you tell somebody who is experiencing prolonged suffering and is wondering why God won't bring it to an end? How do you answer the argument that God's purpose is that we should never be in pain? What was the purpose for Moses' wilderness years?

3. I described the circumstances of Mike, who had found fulfillment from partying, alcohol, and illicit sex before he was saved. He was frustrated because now that he was a Christian, he served the Lord faithfully yet still felt unfulfilled. What was his problem? Why do you think many sincere Christians in the church today aren't fulfilled in life?

4. What would you tell someone who says, "I tried the Christian life and it just doesn't work for me?"

5. Describe the difference between living from self-centered personal strength and from the divine strength of Christ.

6. Read Acts 3:1-12. How was Peter able to make a lame man walk? What are some things you would like to see Jesus do through you?

Chapter 3

THE SECRET OF UNION

Ingredients:
2 family-size tea bags
1 gallon water
2 cups white sugar

Instructions:
Place the tea bags in a small saucepan containing about two cups of water.
Bring to a boil.
Steep for ten minutes, then pour tea concentrate into a gallon pitcher.
While liquid is still very hot, add two cups of sugar. Stir.
Fill gallon pitcher with water and stir.
Serve over ice.

On behalf of everybody in the United States who grew up in the South, I proudly present to you the recipe for *sweet tea*. I have found as I travel that in many parts of the United States and especially abroad, people have been culturally deprived of this delight all of their lives. Try asking a waitress in Pittsburgh for sweet tea. She points at the sugar on the table and then looks at you like you must be blind or something. It's sad; she just doesn't get it. Have you ever watched a person drink Earl Grey tea over a few pieces of ice with no sugar? It's not a pretty sight. And Mexico? The tea there brings to mind the age-old question, "How can a loving God allow such suffering?" Since this is the beverage that will probably be served at the marriage feast of the Lamb, we would all be well advised to learn to enjoy it now! (In Georgia, we think of it as the elixir of the angels.)

A Recipe for Transformation

Seriously, why have I shared the recipe for sweet tea with you? Well, putting aside the obvious culinary mission of mercy, it actually illustrates very clearly the secret I want to share with you in this chapter. God's recipe for transforming us by His grace given in Christ bears some striking similarities to the recipe at the beginning of this chapter.

Turn Up the Heat

The first step in making sweet tea is to turn up the heat so the water will boil. The sugar and tea won't permeate the water unless it is very hot. This is the same way God works in people when He is preparing to reveal a beautiful creation in them. Have you ever noticed how much more receptive you are to Him when the heat is turned up high in your life? When you are in hot water, you usually get into the receiving mode fast! If you have ever asked God to do something powerful in your life, then don't be surprised when trouble comes. He may turn up the heat in your circumstances to prepare you to experience His life. The glory of having Jesus expressing His life through you requires that you pass through the fire. It's not pleasant while it is happening, but when the process is complete the finished product is quite a treat!

The apostle Peter said,

> Beloved, do not be surprised at the fiery ordeal among you, which comes upon you for your testing, as though some strange thing were happening to you; but to the degree that you share the sufferings of Christ, keep on rejoicing, so that also at the revelation of His glory you may rejoice with exultation (1 Peter 4:12-13).

The fire may be hot, but don't despair in your troubles. As the last chapter discussed, God often works in the events of our lives to bring us to the end of confidence in our own ability so He may readily complete His recipe for manifesting the godliness within us.

Add the Sugar and Stir

Unlike cold tea and sugar, hot tea and sugar are totally compatible with each other. In fact, the sugar quickly dissolves when stirred into the hot tea. Once the sugar has dissolved, the very nature of the liquid is changed. The tea and sugar are combined and will never be separated. Their distinct elements have merged together in such a way that they are now one new entity. This isn't the case with iced tea. It is impossible to get sugar to dissolve in tea once it has been served over ice. No matter how much you stir it, the two just won't mix.

When God prepares to manifest the sweet presence of His life within us, He uses heat to cause us to be receptive to His permeating our whole being. It's amazing how hard circumstances can cause us to warm up to His working in our lives.

His indwelling life has transformed our very nature. Just as the sugar and tea have become one, we have been united with our God through Jesus Christ and can never be separated. The apostle Paul wrote, "In love He predestined us to adoption as sons through Jesus Christ to Himself, according to the kind intention of His will, to the praise of the glory of His grace, which He freely bestowed on us in the Beloved" (Ephesians 1:5-6).

Through your adoption in Jesus Christ you have a nature that is in union with God. This union is more than a lofty theological precept. It's a down-to-earth practical reality that can transform the way you live your life every day. It's the realization that our lives aren't independent and separated from the God who created us. To the contrary, our very existence is bound up in Him. There is no God-up-there and you-down-here. You and He are one just as surely as the Father is one with the Son and the Spirit. It is an irreversible, unchangeable union.

I was using the illustration of sweet tea in a Grace Walk Conference once and a man whose field of study was chemistry said, "It is a fact that tea has its own distinct chemical composition and sugar has its own unique chemical composition, but when you put the two together in the way you have described, a totally new chemical composition is created that is neither tea nor sugar." Do you know what it is called? Sweet tea!

The Bible says, "If anyone is in Christ, he is a new creature; the old things passed away; behold, new things have come" (2 Corinthians 5:17). That union is what gives you your identity. When have you ever heard someone refer to tea as "water with tea and sugar in it"? Its nature has been changed; therefore, it is identified by its new identity—*sweet tea.*

Fill the Pitcher with Water

Once the sugar has been placed into the tea, the pitcher must be filled with water. Then the tea is ready to be shared with others. In the Bible, water is a type of the Holy Spirit. The Bible says that the treasure of the life of Jesus is contained in the earthen vessels of our bodies (2 Corinthians 4:7). Yet we must be filled with the Holy Spirit if people are going to be attracted to Christ within us (Ephesians 5:18). To be filled with the Holy Spirit means nothing less than Jesus Christ consuming our total being and expressing His life through us.

It is the Holy Spirit who dwells within our spirit. That same Spirit is the very Spirit of Jesus. His work in joining us to Himself has completely made somebody new of us. We now possess the nature of God. By the death and resurrection of Jesus, God has created a new race of people who possess His nature. Second Peter 1:4 says that through the Spirit of Christ we have "become partakers of the divine nature." Our new nature is a holy nature.

Tea with Sugar Just Isn't the Same

I enjoy sweet tea, but as I've said, I don't like tea with sugar added to it. Some may ask, "Isn't it the same thing?" Not at all. When I'm traveling, I sometimes order iced tea and put sugar in it, but the tea never gets sweet enough for my taste. Sometimes I'll have a glass of iced tea on the table with half an inch of sugar settled at the bottom of the glass. That is tea with sugar, but it's not sweet tea. It is only when the sugar has dissolved in the tea that it receives a sweet nature.

Similarly, there's a difference between Christ merely *being in* my life and Christ *being* my life. Jesus hasn't simply come into our lives. The Bible teaches that He has so filled our being that He is our Life. The very essence of our being has been changed through this supernatural union with Him.

Just as our lives were defined by the first Adam's sinful disobedience, we are now defined by having been joined together with Christ through His incarnation. "As through the one man's disobedience the many were made sinners, even so through the obedience of the One the many will be made righteous" (Romans 5:19). Your righteousness is real because of your union with Righteous Christ. Adam died, and a new identity has become yours in Christ.

If I held up a glass and declared it to be full of sweet tea, someone might argue that it isn't the tea that is sweet, but it's the sugar in the tea. I would disagree. The sugar has so diffused its life into the tea that the nature of the tea has changed. Yes, the tea is sweet because the tea and sugar are one—in union together.

The Bible teaches that we have been made righteous in Christ. Some may argue that it isn't we who are righteous, but rather it is only Jesus within us who is righteous. This is a mistake. We have been made righteous by the union we share with Him. We have His righteous nature!

Paul said, "He made Him who knew no sin to be sin on our behalf, that we might become the righteousness of God in Him" (2 Corinthians 5:21). If you understand your own identity only in terms of Jesus being present in your life, you will fail to understand the radical transformation that took place through His finished work. God didn't just improve your life; He created a brand-new person—one like Jesus!

Many fail to understand the reality of the righteousness that is ours because of our union with Christ. Because they don't feel righteous, they interpret what the Bible says about the matter in a way that falls short of the truth. It is vital to recognize that God took away the unrighteousness we possessed in Adam. You have been given the righteous nature of Jesus.

Those who fail to understand this gift are doomed to a legalistic, works-oriented lifestyle, always trying to achieve righteousness by what they do. Grace is the means by which God has *given* us righteousness. It is not something we have achieved, but rather something that we have received in Christ. Romans 5:17 teaches us that just like we have experienced the abundance of grace we also have received the gift of righteousness.

Janet was witnessing to her friend Christie one day when Christie told her, "I'm really trying to be a Christian." Janet responded, "Christie, you can't try to become a Christian. You can only trust Jesus, believing what God says about what He has done on your behalf. Jesus said, 'It is finished' and He was right. There's nothing left for you to do. Just believe Him!"

Did Janet give an appropriate response to Christie? Of course she did. Yet consider the following remark made by Christie after she became a Christian. "Janet, since I have trusted Christ

I really want to be righteous. I want you to pray for me because I'm trying to be holy so God will be glorified." How should Janet respond to Christie?

Many Christians would tell Christie that they would be praying for her. They might even tell her a few things to do to become holier. Is that an appropriate response? No, it isn't. Christie needs to understand that she is already righteous because of what Christ has done, not because of what she does or doesn't do.

We could say, "Christie, because of Jesus Christ some wonderful things have taken place. First, you have been given eternal life through Jesus. In fact, He is your life. Yet there's more good news than that. He has already made you holy. You don't have to try to be holy in order to become holy. You already are. We want to live holy lives because He has made us holy. Just as Jesus is your life, He is also your righteousness."

The Bible Teaches That We Are Holy

The Bible teaches that we are already holy. It's not something that happens gradually. We may not feel holy or even act holy, but the ultimate authority isn't our own feelings or experiences. The final authority on this matter is the Bible. Consider what God says about the subject in 1 Corinthians 3:16-17:

> Do you not know that you are a temple of God and that the Spirit of God dwells in you? If any man destroys the temple of God, God will destroy Him, for the temple of God is holy, and *that is what you are.*

The Bible presents an irrefutable case in the verse in three simple points. Point one: *You are the temple in which God lives.* Point two: *The temple in which God lives is holy.* Point three: *You are holy!* Either we can believe it, or we might as well take a black marker and strike through this verse in our Bible!

Paul said in Ephesians 4:24 that you are a new person, "which in the likeness of God has been created in righteousness and holiness of the truth." I'll state it again for emphasis: Righteousness is not something we gain by living a certain way. This is the secret of union. It has happened by His grace! Grace always centers on what God has done through Jesus Christ.

Is Our Righteousness Only "Positional"?

For years I couldn't reconcile what I saw taught in the Bible about my righteousness in Christ with my understanding of my own daily experience. I read verses like those already mentioned, but struggled with my own inconsistent behavior. So I took this aspect of truth to be only "positional." My argument went like this: "We aren't literally righteous. God only *sees* us that way. Our *position* is one of righteousness, but our *condition* is that we are unrighteous."

Let's dissect that argument for a minute. We'll get rid of the glaring error first—the idea that God only *sees* us as righteous. Exactly what could this mean? Would one suggest that God sees something that isn't really there? It reminds me of the arrogant professor who saw the unlearned custodian reading his Bible and sneered, "Do you believe that book as it is?" Without hesitation, the custodian replied, "Do you believe it as it ain't?" That's a good question for this matter. Does God see something as it is or as it ain't?

When we consider the argument that our righteousness is positional but not literal we must be intellectually honest. Romans 5:19 corrects the error of believing that we are only positionally righteous:

> As through the one man's disobedience the many
> were made sinners, even so through the obedience
> of the One the many will be made righteous.

This verse very simply presents the truth of our present righteousness in Christ. Paul reminds us that in Adam we all were made to be sinners. In the same way, he says, we have been made righteous in Christ. According to the principles of biblical hermeneutics, we must be consistent in interpreting Scripture. If the last half of this verse means that we are only positionally righteous in Christ, then the first part of the verse must be interpreted to say that we are only positionally sinners in Adam. Were we literally a sinner in Adam or was it only positional? If we were literally sinners then, we are literally righteous now.

Some say that the verse teaches that we will be made righteous when we get to heaven. That's an erroneous idea. People don't become righteous because of their destination in the afterlife. We have become righteous because of being placed into Christ. It's not heaven that makes you righteous—it's Him!

Let's not resist the truth! God says we are righteous because we are in Christ. It is a literal truth. That doesn't mean we always act that way. How we act and who we are may not always coincide. Sometimes I act like a child even though I was born in 1954. Identity isn't determined by what we do but by what He has done by adopting us as His own.

Tea Comes in Many Flavors

Melanie, my wife, often buys a brand of tea called Celestial Seasonings. The package she purchases contains tea bags of different flavors. She likes the Country Apple flavor. I don't care for it, but I do enjoy a flavor called Red Zinger. The apple flavor is boring to me, but the Red Zinger—it's a real eye-opener. When a person is thirsty for some good tea, Red Zinger hits the spot. Melanie disagrees. She thinks the Country Apple is better.

However, it isn't the actual flavor of either tea that satisfies our thirst. As much as we each enjoy our favorite flavors, we have never taken the tea bags out of the box and put them into our mouth to suck the flavor out of the bags. We always add water. The flavor causes the tea to appeal to us, but the water is what really satisfies.

Jesus once said, "If anyone is thirsty, let him come to Me and drink" (John 7:37). Only He can quench the inner thirst for life experienced by every human being. Jesus offers Himself as the only real thirst quencher in this parched world. The way in which He offers His life to the world is ingenious. His life is expressed through many different flavors.

Just as there are many flavors of tea, there is amazing diversity within the body of Christ. There are distinct differences that are obvious. I've met some Country Apples in the body of Christ more than once. I have often seen the distinguished Earl Grey crowd. I have even met a few Red Zingers along the way. Come to think of it, I've encountered just about every flavor you can imagine. I've been with people who have shouted praise and with others who whispered prayers. Some kneel, others stand with their hands lifted, while another group simply bows their heads. Some sing contemporary choruses and others prefer the old hymns. There really are a lot of flavors out there.

Which flavor is the best? It depends on who you ask. The Red Zingers think the Earl Grey crowd is too stuffy, while the Earl Grey crowd believes the Red Zingers are too wild. They both think the Country Apples aren't educated enough, while the apples are convinced that the other groups put far too much confidence in the wisdom of man. This is sort of silly, isn't it? Yet those are the exact attitudes often present in the body of Christ.

God's family is a diverse family. There is a world full of people around us who need to experience the life of Jesus. Like you and me, each person finds certain flavors distasteful and others to be more palatable. The different flavors represent the variety within the church. Contrary to the opinion of many, there is no best flavor. The flavor is not the important element. What really matters is the water. If the pitcher (each of us) is filled with water (Jesus), the flavor (personality) of the tea doesn't really matter.

Some people will be open to Christ's love because of the appeal of one flavor, while others will be more receptive to another. As long as they receive the Water of Life, what difference does the flavor make? The Holy Spirit uses the distinctive flavors found in His church to reach the rest of the world with the great news of His life. Regardless of our own particular flavor, we can each cry out to the world around us, "O taste and see that the LORD is good" (Psalm 34:8)!

WALKING TOGETHER

Dear Father,

Thank You for giving me righteousness through my union with You through Jesus Christ. Renew my mind so I might begin to see myself as You see me. Transform my thoughts to conform to the truth. I acknowledge that You have made me totally righteous in Christ. Cause me to walk in the truth of my identity even when I don't feel like a righteous person. Your life has permeated my being, Lord. By faith I believe it—make it real in my emotions in Your timing.

GROUP QUESTIONS

1. Read 1 Peter 4:12-13. What benefit is to be derived from problems in our lives? What does this passage mean when it talks about "the revelation of His glory"?

2. In 1 Corinthians 6:17, the Bible says that we have been joined together with Christ and made one spirit with Him. What does this mean?

3. What does it mean to be filled with the Spirit (Ephesians 5:18)?

4. What would you say to a person who says, "I am trying to be righteous"? What verses from the Bible would you show him?

5. What is the difference between positional righteousness and literal righteousness? Which viewpoint do you believe?

6. Just as there are many flavors of tea, so there are believers with diverse personalities and styles. Which one is the best? Describe the flavor you prefer. List three positive aspects of a flavor you don't particularly like.

Chapter 4

THE SECRET OF A
RELIGION-FREE LIFESTYLE

"I want to be a better husband," Carl said to me while glancing over at his wife, Katie. "I know I have an explosive temper, and I really do try to control it," he continued. As he spoke, Katie sat by his side, slightly turned away from him. Tears pooled in her eyes as she listened to him talk. Finally she spoke. "Steve, I don't doubt he tries to control his temper. But the bottom line is, he isn't succeeding, and I'm getting tired of his sarcastic criticism."

The people before me were Christians—dedicated people who truly wanted to do the right thing. They even had a son about to go away to college to prepare for the ministry. Yet I have never met two people who were more defeated. In spite of all the outward indicators of successful Christian lives, their marriage had hit rock-bottom. They would have received a grade of A-plus if they had been scored on their religious commitment, but their marriage would have received a failing grade for sure.

Carl had never been physically abusive to his wife, but his verbal abuse had driven her to the place of despair. He had promised repeatedly to change the impatient, critical demeanor he had toward her. I believed he sincerely wanted to overcome the sin of anger, but he just couldn't do it. With all of his good intentions, self-imposed religious rules, and promises to God, he was still enslaved to a sin from which he could not experience freedom.

Methods for Overcoming Sins

As I listened to Carl explain his despair over his inability to control his temper and his tongue, I asked him how he had approached the problem until now. He told how he had read religious books about overcoming anger. Some mornings he would awaken and promise himself that he wouldn't say anything critical regardless of how he felt about Katie's actions that day. He would even ask God to help him be patient. "Those are usually our worst days," he said with obvious desperation. He had memorized Bible verses dealing with patience and love. In an effort to suppress his feelings, he would often quote the verses when he felt angry. But none of these methods seemed to work. Nothing seemed to work.

In the weeks to come, Carl would discover that his impasse with his own anger was a result of the methods he used to deal with it. The problem wasn't that he used the wrong methods. The reason for his unending defeat was that he believed victory over sin could come through a *method*. He believed that a dedicated religious approach to overcoming his problem should work. But it didn't.

Contrary to what many sincere followers of Christ believe, victory over sin doesn't come by finding and practicing the right religious method, even if it's one we think is from the Bible. Rather, victory is found in the Person of Jesus Christ. The apostle Paul said that God "gives us the victory through our Lord

Jesus Christ" (1 Corinthians 15:57). No religious method will give real victory over sin.

Even if Carl had been able to suppress the expression of his anger, it would have found an outlet in some other way. Maybe he would have become depressed. Maybe he would have become bitter toward Katie. Or maybe he would have become proud of being a good person, so good that he could overcome anger. He simply would have traded one kind of sin for another.

Trying to overcome sin by changing one's behavior is typical of a person who still thinks religious methods are the answer. There's a big problem with religious methods—they all revolve around religious rules. Another word, and one often used in the Bible for rules, is the word *law*.

Law is a system in which somebody tries to make spiritual progress or gain God's blessings based on what he or she does. The focus is always on religious commitment and religious rules. It's nothing more than dead religion.

There is a secret about religion that you may find surprising or even hard to believe. It's this: *God hasn't called you to religion. Jesus didn't come for that.* The world was up to its neck in religion before He came into this world. The last thing we needed was for Him to come and start a new religion.

Religion is the attempt people make to jump through moral hoops they imagine that God is holding. They wrongly think that if they can just do the right things, He will be pleased with them. The sad thing is that it's all an exercise in futility. Jesus wouldn't have had to come if religion offered a workable solution. It never has and never will. Only He is the answer.

Victory over sin can never come by ramping up our religious performance. Driving faster makes no difference at all if you're headed in the wrong direction. Our direction is to be toward dependence on the Christ who lives inside us, not on making good mileage in changing our own behavior.

If it's not by religious devotion, how do we overcome sin?

How can we be truly changed? It is experienced by the expression of the indwelling Christ. The absence of expressed sin is not victory. Jesus Christ within us is our victory. Until you understand that it isn't your relationship to religion but to Him that counts, your default setting will be a legalistic lifestyle. It will never be more than a lifestyle that revolves around rules. Take my word for it—there is no rut like a religious rut. Thank God, Jesus came to get you out of all that.

Committing Spiritual Adultery

Let's think about adultery for a moment. Why adultery? It's because that's what goes on in the lives of religious people every day. I'm not talking about physical adultery—people cheating on their mates. This is worse than that. This is a kind of adultery where a person cheats on Jesus Christ. It doesn't get any worse than that. We will call it "spiritual adultery."

What comes to your mind when you read the words *spiritual adultery*? Many would suggest that spiritual adultery occurs when we sin. Good guess, but that answer doesn't go far enough. Spiritual adultery can exist in the life of a person who is committing no known sins. Paul describes its meaning in Romans 7:1-4:

> Do you not know, brethren (for I am speaking to those who know the law), that the law has jurisdiction over a person as long as he lives? For the married woman is bound by law to her husband while he is living; but if her husband dies, she is released from the law concerning the husband. So then, if while her husband is living she is joined to another man, she shall be called an adulteress; but if her husband dies, she is free from the law, so that she is not an adulteress though she is joined to another man. Therefore, my brethren, you also were made to die to the Law through the body of Christ, so that you might be joined to another, to Him who was raised from the dead, in order that we might bear fruit for God.

A Word About the Law of God

Paul uses the model of marriage to teach about the relationship between the Christian and rules. He pointed the Roman Christians to their own laws by reminding them that if a woman was married to a man, she was bound to him as long as he lived. If she left him for another man she became an adulteress, because the only way out of a marriage was by death. They all knew that law well.

Let's pause here to establish something important about the Law of God. It has nothing to do with you. In fact, it never has. The Law was given to ancient Israel for the purpose of exposing her religious arrogance. The Israelites believed that, given the right direction, they could do exactly what God wanted and thus gain His constant favor. Yahweh wanted them to see otherwise by knowing that their problem wasn't a head problem but a heart problem. They didn't need a new understanding. What they needed was a new nature.

For that reason, He gave them the Law for the purpose of stimulating sin in their lives to shake them out of their smug self-righteousness. Romans 5:20 explains: "God's law was given so that all people could see how sinful they were" (NLT).

The Law wasn't given to anybody except Israel. Psalm 147:19-20 says, "He has revealed his word to Jacob, his laws and decrees to Israel. He has done this for no other nation; they do not know his laws" (NIV).

Nobody today still lives under the Old Testament Law. That covenant was made obsolete when Jesus died. In Hebrews 8:13, we are told, "When He [God] said, 'A new covenant,' He has made the first obsolete. But whatever is becoming obsolete and growing old is ready to disappear."

The Old Covenant of religious-rules-keeping that was given to Israel to show them their self-righteousness no longer exists. It has disappeared and been made obsolete because of the finished work of Jesus Christ at the cross. He has inaugurated a

New Covenant of grace. The cross is *the* defining point that marks the beginning of the covenant of grace.

Before that time, Israel was under the Law. That was a painful place to be because the Law did one thing perfectly. It ministered death and condemnation to those who lived under it. In fact, Paul called the Law a ministry of death and condemnation (see 2 Corinthians 3:7-9).

It isn't the Law that is dead today. The Law of God is eternal. What is dead is us! We have been crucified with Christ (see Galatians 2:20) and have no relationship to the Law whatsoever. Gentiles never did, but now even the Jews have been released from the Law. Paul wrote, "Now, by dying to what once bound us, we have been released from the law so that we serve in the new way of the Spirit, and not in the old way of the written code."

Nag, Nag, Nag!

The problem that still exists is that people *think* they are supposed to live by religious rules (the Law). So away they go, trying to keep rules that don't even apply to them. In that wrong place, they soon discover that the Law will still do what it always did to the Jews—bring a sense of condemnation and failure.

Imagine being in a relationship with somebody who criticizes your every move. After a while, we grow weary of a mate who always critiques every move we make. We find ourselves wanting to lash out, pointing out his or her faults. Yet there is a problem when a person tries to do that to the Law: He has no faults. In fact, the psalmist said that "the law of the Lord is perfect" (Psalm 19:7).

Although perfect, Mr. Law shows no compassion whatsoever. He tells us everything to do, but won't lift a finger to help us. He is quick to point it out when we fail. His whole demeanor in relating to us is one of condemnation and death. That's what it's like when we think and act as if our lives are to be governed by religious rules.

It was a miserable existence, but there was nothing Israel could do to get out of the relationship. Marriage is "until death do us part," and the Law is never going to die. They were stuck in the rules rut.

Meanwhile, in eternity, God looked down on His helpless and hopeless people. He was thinking how much He would like for not just Israel but all humanity to be joined to Him. "Oh, if I were married to you, I would treat you differently," He might say. "I would simply love you and wouldn't be demanding like Mr. Law has been."

Yet the problem remained. Israel was born married to Law. So from the eternal vantage point, God devised a plan. In order to get the Israelites out of the marriage to Law and, even greater, to bring all of us into grace, He planned and carried out a death. It wasn't Law that died, but instead, God worked it out so we all died. How did that happen?

It happened in the person of Jesus Christ. His incarnation was God's act in redeeming not only Israel but also all of mankind. Jesus moved in among us so we could live among the Father, Son, and Holy Spirit. He took every one of us and bound us up in Himself. The Last Adam refused to stop short of delivering us from the bondage we experienced as a result of the first Adam's failure. He wasn't about to allow the dirty deed of the first Adam to supersede His own righteous act.

Jesus took you into Himself in such a way that His obedience to the Father was your obedience. His death was your death. His burial, resurrection, and ascension were yours! In other words, His was a *vicarious* life and death. He acted as *you* when He came as a man. He took our place in every way needed to bring humanity to His Father.

Paul must have hardly been able to contain himself when he wrote the good news (gospel) in Romans 7:4 that we died through the body of Christ so we might be joined to Jesus! There are no rules for you to keep! Jesus has done away with that system altogether! There is nothing for you to do to make yourself acceptable to God. That may be the focus of religion, but Jesus has set you free from that too! The only thing you need to do—the only thing you *can* do—is simply believe the truth of the gospel. Jesus has done it all. We simply willfully participate in His victory through faith in Him!

We aren't married to the Law. We are married to Christ Jesus. He always acts in love toward us. He is thrilled that we are His. The groom wants just one thing from His bride—that she eagerly receive His love! Anything He calls upon us to do, He ends up doing Himself! (See 1 Thessalonians 5:24.) If He ever asks us to carry a burden, He sweeps us off our feet and carries us! Ephesians 1:7-8 says that He has lavished the riches of His grace upon us. He never condemns us (Romans 8:1), but always affirms and lovingly guides us. He anticipates the eternal honeymoon He will enjoy with us.

Not all is always perfect in our experience of this marriage made in heaven, however. Sometimes you may be confused about your role as the bride of Christ. It is true that at the cross, the old you died with Him. Now you are a brand-new person. Paul said you are "a new creature" and that "the old things passed away" (2 Corinthians 5:17). However, despite the fact that you are new in nature, you still have the same brain in your skull. If you don't understand the fact that you have no relationship to the Law, there will be an inclination to attempt to relate to Mr. Grace (Jesus) as if He were Mr. Law. The sad thing is that this is exactly what religion tells us to do.

If we don't understand our identity in Christ we might ask, "Jesus, what do You want me to do?" To which He could respond, "I want you to believe Me and receive and enjoy My love!" "Yes," we might answer, "but what do You want me to do?" "I want you to receive My love," He could again say. "I understand that part, Lord. But what do You want me to *do*?"

Do you see where the problem arises? Until you know that

you have no relationship to the Law, you will attempt to relate to Jesus through the law system or religious rules-keeping. That will never work. God's primary concern is not your doing, but your being. He knows that when you understand who you are, then the doing of the Christian life will naturally flow from that revelation. Grace focuses on being, while Law focuses on keeping religious rules.

Reviewing where he had come from in his own life as a devout rules-keeping Jewish leader, Paul wrote,

> We know very well that we are not set right with God by rule-keeping but only through personal faith in Jesus Christ. How do we know? We tried it—and we had the best system of rules the world has ever seen! Convinced that no human being can please God by self-improvement, we believed in Jesus as the Messiah so that we might be set right before God by trusting in the Messiah, not by trying to be good (Galatians 2:16 MSG).

Paul abandoned the religion of the Law and spent the rest of his life sharing the good news of grace. In his own words, "What actually took place is this: I tried keeping rules and working my head off to please God, and it didn't work. So I quit being a 'law man' so that I could be God's man" (Galatians 2:19 MSG).

How Adultery Happens

Sometimes we're so used to rules that the very idea of living without religious restrictions scares us. It reminds me of what Red told Andy Dufresne about the prison walls in *The Shawshank Redemption*, the movie based on a Stephen King story: "These walls are funny. First you hate 'em, then you get used to 'em. Enough time passes, you get so you depend on them. That's institutionalized."

Many of us have some acquaintance with that, don't we? It's

interesting that the word *religion* likely comes from a Latin word that actually means "to bind." A positive spin could be put on it that suggests religion binds people together to each other or God, but that wouldn't be true. It's Jesus who does that. Religion only binds us to rules and the never-ending demand to perform better. It's a prison sentence, for sure—"but now we have been released from the law, for we died to it and are no longer captive to its power" (Romans 7:6 NLT). Don't allow yourself to be institutionalized by dead religion.

When somebody gets frustrated because Jesus won't give him a list of rules, he may turn back to Law and ask, "Will you tell me what to do?" Mr. Law is always ready to make a connection with wandering eyes—eyes that look away from Jesus. So it's possible then to find oneself married to Mr. Grace (Jesus) and yet involved again with Mr. Law.

What is it called when a person is married to one partner but involved with another? Spiritual adultery. That's exactly what happens when people try to build their lives around religious rules. The Bible clearly teaches that we are dead to the law. We have no relationship with religious rules—none. Jesus Christ defines our lives.

What Will Make Me Behave?

Some find it scary to think they are totally free from a system of rules. When I first began to understand grace I was afraid I might become derelict in my responsibilities. I even thought that without rules, I might begin to minimize the seriousness of sin in my own life. Maybe even become an example of "Grace Gone Wild!"

I came to discover I had found security in my religious rules. When I kept them, I felt everything was all right with me spiritually. When I sensed any sort of spiritual deficit in my life, I would mentally run down the checklist of rules to see which one I was failing. But when a person examines himself to see if he is living up to the Law, he will always discover areas of inconsistency. I thought the answer was to renew my efforts to do more. Yet even when I poured my energies into keeping these self-imposed laws, I wasn't really experiencing the life God intends. The rules-keeping lifestyle revolves around religion, not relationship—and you are *made* for relationship.

The apostle Paul walked the same legalistic road as many of us. He mentioned how he had believed that he could experience life to the fullest if he only did the right things. Yet he said that when he embraced any commandment in order to find life, it "proved to result in death for me" (Romans 7:10). There is no list of rules a person can follow and experience life. You may sometimes think the reason for your frustration is because you don't adequately live up to certain rules, but the real problem is focusing on rules at all. Life is not about that—never has been.

Galatians 3:21-22 says,

> If a law had been given which was able to impart life, then righteousness would indeed have been based on the law. But the Scripture has shut up everyone under sin, so that the promise by faith in Jesus Christ might be given to those who believe.

It is important to remember that living by law doesn't necessarily mean that you focus on the Law found in Scripture. Like the Pharisees, many people have gone beyond the Bible and created their own laws. A lifestyle ruled by law is one where the focus is on performance. It is a lifestyle that is obsessed with doing the right thing instead of obsessed with Jesus. It is religion. You're probably familiar with it. I hope you're getting motivated toward a religion-free lifestyle as you read this chapter.

Stay Off the Law Tree

When God placed Adam and Eve in the Garden of Eden, He specifically told them not to eat from the tree of the knowledge of good and evil. They were to eat from the tree of life, which represents Jesus Christ—who is life. Yet man chose to disobey and eat from the forbidden tree. The tree of the knowledge of good and evil could be called "the law tree" because it offered knowledge about the rules of right and wrong. When Adam ate from that tree, he instantly found himself at a place where doing right and avoiding wrong became the preeminent issue of life. Until that point, his behavior had always glorified God because he had walked with the Lord daily, depending entirely on Him for every detail in life. Now his focus was on his behavior, not God.

Does that sound familiar? It's the template that frames every religion in the world, even the "Christian religion." Authentic Christianity has nothing to do with that but has everything to do with living out of the union with God discussed in chapter 3.

Jesus came to rectify the damage caused by Adam's sin. Until the fall, the only thing that mattered was that Adam and Eve were living in total dependence on God. After their sin, their primary focus was set on doing the right things. Through the cross, however, we have been restored to the place Adam forfeited. As a result, the criterion for our lives returns to God's original design: living in total dependence on Him at every moment. In Christ, our innocence before God has been reestablished. We don't need rules! When a person focuses on doing right and avoiding wrong, they are completely missing the point of the cross as it relates to their lifestyle. They are functioning from the law tree, not life.

Doing Good Can Be a Sin

In order to better understand what it means for a person's lifestyle when they are trapped in religion, consider this illustration: Pretend that one morning, after he had eaten from the law tree, Adam woke up because his wife, Eve, was leaning over him and kissing him gently on the cheek. "Good morning, my sweetheart," she whispered. "I brought you breakfast in bed this morning. You seemed to be resting so well that I let you sleep late today."

Adam opened his eyes, took one look at Eve, and snarled at her in anger, "What do you mean waking me up, woman? Couldn't you see that I was asleep? How dare you! What have you shoved under my nose…a bowl of fruit? You've already caused me enough trouble with fruit! Get out of my face!" Shocked, Eve's eyes filled with tears and she ran off to a secluded place where she could cry alone.

By mid-morning Adam was feeling guilty about how he had treated his wife. He found her and humbly approached her. "Eve, I am so sorry. It was so wrong for me to behave that way. It was simply evil! Please forgive me. I wouldn't blame you if you left me for another…well, anyway, you get the point." Eve looked up through teary eyes as Adam continued. "Eve, I'm going to make it up to you, I promise.

"Tomorrow will be your special day. Listen, world! Tomorrow is Eve Day on Planet Earth," he shouted. True to his word, the next day Adam treated Eve like a queen. He pampered her all day long. That night when she went to bed, he gently leaned across her, kissed her on the cheek, and said, "Good night, my dear princess. I'm so blessed to have you as my wife."

"Oh Adam, you're so good to me," she cooed.

Now let's see how much we understand about religious legalism. There are only two questions on this test. Our answers to these questions will reveal whether we tend to see life primarily through a religious lens or through the filter of a loving relationship to God. Ready?

1. Was God pleased with Adam's actions on the first day in the story?

2. Was God pleased with Adam's actions on the second day in the story?

The answer to both questions is no. God was not pleased on either day. Adam's behavior was evil on the first day and good on the second day. However, we must recognize that the tree of the knowledge of good and evil can be the source of good as well as evil. Although Adam's behavior changed from one day to the next, he still had the same problem. On both days he was up the wrong tree!

When religion governs your life, your focus is on improving your behavior. Yet even if you do manage to improve it, what have you accomplished spiritually? Jesus didn't give the gift of salvation simply to help us perform better. He came to earth so we might have an abundant life! (see John 10:10).

There are many miserable people, both believers and unbelievers, who have exemplary behavior. But joy in life doesn't come by doing the right thing. The secret of a religion-free lifestyle is to experience Jesus at every moment, free from demanding religious rules. It's a lifestyle motivated by desire, not duty. It's love, not laws, that God wants to guide us in how we live our lives.

Even if you do good, your actions may still be sin. Only those actions that are animated by the life of Jesus within you have real value. When we live in total dependence on His indwelling life, we are walking in faith and will always glorify God. When we focus on improving our behavior, we are not walking in faith. That's the essence of dead religion.

Hebrews 11:6 plainly says, "Without faith it is impossible to please Him." The Bible says that whatever is not of faith is sin. So a person may do something good and his action could still be a sin because it isn't done in faith. Someone has rightly said that God doesn't appreciate what He doesn't initiate—and He certainly isn't the one who gave birth to religion.

You Don't Need Religious Rules

Paul clearly asserted that we were made to die to the law so we could be joined to Christ. What relationship do we have, then, to a system of rules that govern behavior? Absolutely none! You were "made to die to the Law through the body of Christ, that you might be joined to another, to Him who was raised from the dead" (Romans 7:4). Having been given the resurrection life of Jesus Christ, you don't need the law anymore. You have Jesus Christ living within to guide your steps.

"Don't we need to commit ourselves to the laws of God?" a person might ask. That's like asking if we should commit ourselves to someone other than our own mate. *We have died to the rules system.*

My wife, Melanie, and I have four children, all adults now. In the places where we lived while rearing them, there were laws governing the responsibilities of parents. These laws are a part of the penal code to ensure that children receive proper care. If parents break these laws, there is the risk that their children will be taken out of their home. In fact, if a violation of the law is severe enough, the parents might even go to jail.

I must confess that during all our years of child-rearing, we never went to the courthouse to read those laws on the books. There are probably hundreds of laws concerning parental responsibilities recorded there, but we've never read even one. One might wonder if we weren't afraid we might break the law and have our children taken away from us. Yet that thought never crossed our minds once.

I didn't need laws about parenting to dictate how I reared my children. That has nothing to do with us. Do you know why? It's because we have related to our children on the basis of love! Love for Andrew, Amy, David, and Amber caused us to care for them in a way that far surpasses the minimum requirements of the law. I suppose somebody could argue that we kept the laws about child-rearing, but I'd resist that observation. I'd say, "No, we didn't. What we did had nothing to do with the law. We neither kept nor broke the law because our parenting didn't function in that realm."

To experience the secret of a religion-free lifestyle is to know that your actions will be motivated by love for Jesus Christ. The driving force of your life won't be duty, but desire. You will crawl out from under the heavy weight of *ought to* and start living from a *want to* motivation. You won't have a reckless disregard for religious laws. You simply won't have *any* regard for religious laws. What does *that* have to do with you? Nothing!

That kind of statement might startle some people. "Antinomianism!" some theologian might cry. (For the rest of us, the word simply describes one who is against law.) I don't advocate being against the laws of God, but merely want to point out that the law has nothing to do with us anymore. *We live in Christ Jesus.*

Why Do We Still Live by Rules?

The Bible clearly teaches that we died to the Law: that system of religious rules-keeping. Why, then, do so many people today still try to build a lifestyle around rules? Paul deals with this question and bluntly answers it in Colossians 2:20-23:

> If you have died with Christ to the elementary principles of the world, why, as if you were living in the world, do you submit yourself to decrees, such as, "Do not handle, do not taste, do not touch!" (which all refer to things destined to perish with use)—in accordance with the commandments and teachings of men? These are matters which have, to be sure, the appearance of wisdom in self-made religion and self-abasement and severe treatment of the body, but are of no value against fleshly indulgence.

Here Paul asks a pointed question that presses hard those who embrace religion. He begins by again emphasizing that we have died to the religious rules system. Remember, the Bible calls it "obsolete." This is the same point Paul made in Romans

7:4, when he declared we were made to die to the law in the body of Christ so we might be released from law and joined to Him.

The next question is an obvious one that demands an answer from many in the contemporary church: *Why are you acting like you are a part of that system by submitting yourself to all these regulations?* How would you answer that question? Do you understand now that through Jesus Christ, God has set you free from the rules system so you can experience Him as your life? If so, why do you think you still need rules?

As I explained this biblical truth to a fellow named Hank, he argued, "But Steve, you don't understand! God gave us His law and we must obey it! Without God's laws, people would run wild!" Hank's concern reflected a common misunderstanding about what happens when we believe the gospel. He failed to recognize that believers don't *want* to run wild. Our awareness and appreciation of the presence of Jesus within us changes our desires!

If you think you can live a lifestyle of habitual sin without giving it a thought, you will ultimately find yourself suffocating in its stinking stench. It is momentarily exciting to run into the sin house, but if you are a follower of Jesus, you will soon find yourself inwardly screaming, "I've got to get out of here!"

So why do many Christians live by laws? In Colossians 2:23, Paul says it is because "these are matters which have, to be sure, the appearance of wisdom in self-made religion..." Those who don't live a religion-free lifestyle love religious rules for one simple reason—it makes them look good. It's all about appearance. If you're a religious person, you enjoy the special status you hold among your peers when you seem to keep all the right rules. It is a matter of pride. We may call it our "testimony" or our "reputation" or our "witness," but the truth, plain and simple, is that conformity to religious rules creates acceptance and approval from others in the religious community. It also gives us a prideful, false sense of value based on how we live.

It is interesting to discover that among the various camps of religious legalism, different sets of rules are held in high esteem. One group is known by the things they do, while another group is known by the things they don't do. Yet in each clan, those held in highest regard are the ones who are the best at keeping the particular esoteric rules of their group. The sad irony of their diligent focus on behavior is that their rules "are of no value against fleshly indulgence" (Colossians 3:23). In other words, a ton of rules don't provide an ounce of prevention against sin. To the contrary, religious rules actually impede our spiritual walk in a way that most people would never imagine.

The secret of a religion-free lifestyle will bring you into the freedom of walking with Jesus. Don't settle for an adulterous relationship with a cheap imitation. The One who loves you wants your affection and devotion to be only for Him. Walk away from religion and fall into the arms of Jesus.

 WALKING TOGETHER

Dear Father,

I realize I have misunderstood how You have designed for me to live my life. I have been focusing on being a devoted religious person. Unintentionally, I have committed spiritual adultery. Now I see the truth that You have set me free from the demands of religion so I can experience and fully enjoy Your life. I affirm that I am dead to that law-filled, religious-rules-keeping system and am married to Jesus. Teach me to allow my lifestyle to flow from my relationship to You. I love You, Jesus. Renew my mind in this area so I might walk in the complete freedom You have already given me through the cross.

✼ GROUP QUESTIONS

1. At the beginning of the chapter, I described Carl's predicament with his anger. None of the methods he tried seemed to work. Discuss some of the common methods people use to try to overcome sins. Having read this chapter, what would you tell Carl about his problem with anger?

2. Read Romans 7:1-5. What is spiritual adultery? What relationship does the believer have to religious rules? Describe ways that you have committed spiritual adultery. How can we know for sure that we have no relationship to Mr. Law?

3. Describe the process that leads to committing spiritual adultery.

4. How can it be a sin to do a good thing? Describe the differences between the law tree and the life tree.

5. Do you need the Law? Why or why not? If we don't live by religious rules, what will ensure that we don't live a sinful lifestyle?

6. Read Colossians 2:20-23. Why do some people try to build their lifestyle around a set of rules? List some rules you have embraced in your own life.

Chapter 5

THE SECRET OF DOING WHAT WE WANT

"Lord, I don't understand myself. I honestly want to be a godly husband and dad. What's wrong with me? I can't even do the most basic things necessary to be a good Christian!" The year was 1988. These were the words I wrote in my journal on January 16. I remember well my frustration. Actually, it was more than frustration. At the time, I loathed myself because of the inconsistency I saw in my life.

A few weeks earlier I had done what I had always done at the beginning of a new year. I wrote my new year's resolutions. My commitments at the beginning of every new year always included promises to myself about spiritual disciplines for the coming year. One of my promises for that year was that I would read the Bible and pray with my family *every single day* of the year, without fail. I had reasoned that, unlike previous years, this time I *really* meant it. I would do it this time. I *must* do it this time!

Yet here I was less than three weeks later, having neglected for the past two days the very thing I had *promised* I would not miss for 365 days. Failing to have devotional time with my family every day was just one of the areas where I struggled with consistency. It seemed that every time I identified an area where I wanted to improve my Christian life, things seemed to get worse instead of better. My failure seemed to always be in direct proportion to my efforts to succeed.

Sin's Secret Power

There is a little-known reason why we find ourselves feeling like we've failed after having tried with such sincerity to live a life that honors God. It is almost as if Satan has a secret weapon that we don't know about. It's not uncommon to start moving forward with perfectly pure intentions and with a proper motivation, and then suddenly find ourselves lying flat on our back on the spiritual battlefield. When I resolved to pray and read the Bible with my family every day, I was totally sincere. Yet within three weeks, I felt like I was shot down. Can you relate to the experience of earnestly setting out to do what you think you need to do, only to soon find yourself defeated? You may be thrilled to learn the secret I'll tell you in this chapter.

What is that secret? It is the secret of doing what you want. Before you get mad and throw down this book, hear me out. I'm not saying that sinning is okay or that it doesn't matter what you do. Behavior does matter. You'll see that as you keep reading this chapter. What I *am* saying is that most people don't really *know* what they want. They think that if they were to give in to their wants, they would go wild with unrestrained sins. The irony of that belief is that when they do something that doesn't align with their true identity in Christ now, they experience an internal conflict over it. Why? *Because it's not what they truly want to do!*

Fleshly impulses may provoke you to do wrong, but deep down inside, the real you doesn't want to do those things. If you did, you could spend the rest of your life living a hedonistic, I-couldn't-care-less sort of lifestyle and it wouldn't bother you at all. But that's not who you are.

Because most people don't know their identity in Christ, their thinking is wrong. They believe that because temptation has an appeal, they must refuse to do what they want to do. Therefore they live in constant self-imprisonment. But what if it were true that your deepest desires aren't to do wrong things, but to do the things God wants you to do? Well, that's the case.

The problem is that, because people don't know their authentic desires, they run to the religious rules discussed in the last chapter for shelter. What they don't know is that those rules don't help at all but instead hurt them.

Law is the Trojan horse that has infiltrated contemporary Christendom, with devastating results. Religious rules *look* so compatible with the Christian life that many never suspect their deadly effect until they become victims. Most people fail to see the enemy approaching because he is dressed up in such an attractive suit of clothes, which constitute the Law. Yet beneath the moral veneer of his appearance lies a sinister force that catches the unsuspecting off guard.

Now, don't get the idea that I am demeaning the place of law. It served its purpose with Israel well. The trouble is that if you try to connect to it today, it will have the same effect on you it did them.

What does the law do in somebody's life? It surprises many to discover that rules don't curb sin; they stir it up. Romans 5:20 says, "The Law came in so that the transgression would increase." Have you believed God gave the law so people would keep it? That is not its purpose. The Bible clearly teaches that the purpose of the law was to reveal sin to the religiously arrogant nation of ancient Israel. Law doesn't *generate* sin, but it does most definitely *stimulate* it within any person who embraces it. It brings it from beneath the surface right out into the open.

First Corinthians 15:56 tells us that "the power of sin is the law." Rules don't keep you from sinning; they *cause* you to sin!

So the unwitting person who wants to please God and then determines to build his or her life around spiritual rules is asking for a lifestyle filled with failure! There certainly is nothing wrong with a man praying and reading the Bible with his family, but when I wrote my own ten commandments at the beginning of each new year, I immediately set myself up for failure. Law didn't care how sincere I was when I wrote, "Thou shalt have family altar every day this year." Law still did its job, and 16 days later it was all over except the crying.

Stepping Back Through Time

Consider the origin of the codified Law of God. While the matrix for the Law system can be seen in the Garden of Eden at the tree of the knowledge of good and evil, the written laws were not given until Mount Sinai. Why did God give His written Law to man? Since He is omniscient, it isn't possible that He thought they would keep it. So if He knew that man wasn't going to keep His laws before He even gave them, why did He do it?

Allow me to take literary liberty at this point by asking you to use your imagination. This scenario reveals the behind-the-scenes story of why God ever gave the Law. It's not in the Bible, but it illustrates the heart of an independent, proud people and the heart of their loving God. Let's step back to a time in history when man is whining to God about his inability to please Him by his behavior. The conversation might have gone like this:

"Lord, it seems we can't please You regardless of what we do. What do You want from us?"

"I want you to trust Me and allow Me to guide you moment by moment," God answered.

"God, we have the cause of this problem figured out. If You will just tell us what to *do*, then we can do it and everything will be okay."

"No," answered God, "it isn't a matter of your doing. The issue is one of *trusting*. Just trust Me."

"No, Lord. Just give us a list of rules. What would it take to be right with You?"

"I don't want to give you a list. I want you to trust Me," God answered.

"Lord, give us the list!" Israel demanded.

"I would really prefer that you simply trust Me," God answered again.

"Give us the list. Tell us what to do! Just tell us what to do!" they insisted.

Isn't this the depiction of Old Testament Israel's life? Finally there came a point in time when God gave the written law. "I've jotted down a few things here that reflect My eternal purity," He told the people.

"Give them to us! We will do them. Finally, we will know what to *do*. Give us the list. Give it here."

So on Mount Sinai God handed Israel the Law through the prophet Moses. Looking at the demands of the Law, Israel immediately responded, "We can't do that!"

"Exactly," God replied.

God didn't think for one moment that they would keep the Law. Remember, He knows everything. He didn't give the Law because *He* believed man would keep it, but rather because *man* believed he could keep it. Man mistakenly thought that if he had clear instructions, he could achieve a righteous standing with God on the basis of his behavior. So God gave the law to demonstrate that righteousness can never come by adherence to religious rules. The Law is intended to bring frustration to the point of despair—despair that leads to giving up all hope in the ability to successfully live in a way that pleases God.

The Law isn't for us today, but if we dance with the Law, it will force us to see our own inability to accomplish a righteous lifestyle, just like it did with Israel. The purpose of the Law was to inflame sin, thus causing Israel to see her own hopeless state apart from the mercy and grace of God.

Legalistic Discipleship

Every Christian understands that it is impossible to experience salvation by keeping religious rules. Yet many believe that once a person becomes a Christian, the strategy changes. Let's walk through the commonly used approach in leading Carla to faith in Christ and then starting to "disciple" her after her conversion.

"Carla, you simply need to trust Jesus to experience salvation. That's all that is necessary. What? Stop your bad habits? No, Carla. You don't understand. You don't need to do anything to be saved. Just trust Jesus. What? Start attending church? No, my friend! Just place your faith in Christ and receive Him. Clean up your language? Carla, you're missing the point. This isn't about what *you* do; it is about what *He* has already done. Becoming a Christian is *all* Him! Just trust Him. Just believe. It's by faith, Carla. It's not through doing anything. It's Him alone!"

Then Carla trusts Christ and begins to walk with Him…

"God bless you, Carla! I am so glad you've trusted Christ. Now that you're a Christian, I know you want to get started right, don't you? Let me tell you a few things that will help you get started in your Christian life. First, you must to come to church Sunday morning and let the pastor know you have been saved. Then you have to be baptized and join the church. You should attend all the services, including Sunday night and Wednesday night. You also ought to become a part of the women's prayer group. And our outreach visitation on Tuesdays too. Can you sing? If so, you really ought to join the choir. Oh, don't forget our home study group. And here's an absolute *must*, Carla—you need to get into the Bible. Read three chapters in the Old Testament and two in the New and you'll go through your whole Bible every year that way. And don't forget about prayer—you should pray about 30 minutes every morning. Oh yes, did I mention tithing?…"

Is it any wonder that the Carlas we reach ultimately go running out the back door of the church world when nobody is watching? We *say* we recognize the Christian life is a walk in grace, but our approach to discipleship often reveals a not-so-subtle legalism that ultimately sucks the vitality out of new Christians. Serving as a local church pastor for over 20 years, I saw many people press the eject button and disappear from church a short time after receiving Christ. Others who remained ended up looking like they had had a legalism lobotomy. They still went through the motions of Christian living, but without any sense of life in their activity.

When you understand your God-given, Christ-sourced identity, you won't need a religious Gestapo to police your actions or dictate your behavior. You will learn that the One who lives inside you is the One who generates the desire to live a godly lifestyle. As you grow in grace, you will learn to distinguish temptations to do wrong that neither originate from you nor reflect your core desires.

Discipleship is important, but biblical discipleship means strengthening a person in an understanding of what it means to be in Christ, not carrying out an indoctrination in religious rules. Teach a new believer who she is in Christ, and she will awaken to desires grounded in her true self. Tell her she "can't do this" and is "supposed to do that" and you set her up for spiritual ruin. We weren't called to a spiritual list, but rather to a spiritual rest. Jesus said that those who come to Him would receive rest (see Matthew 11:28). That kind of statement scares legalists; they immediately become afraid that if a person embraces a position of freedom in Christ, he or she might go wild.

Grace Creates Godly Desires

Legalistic discipleship emphasizes *obligation* in what is

libelously called "the Christian life." It stresses what a person must do and must avoid. It completely misses the fact that it isn't duty but desire that causes one walking in grace to behave. Paul told those in Rome, "Though you were slaves of sin, you became obedient *from the heart* to that form of teaching to which you were committed" (Romans 6:17).

If you get in touch with your true desires—the ones defined by the Christ who is your very life—you will discover that you don't need to be coerced into this or that behavior. You will connect with a freedom to live your lifestyle based on the God-given desires that flow from the life of Jesus, who lives inside you. Grace focuses on *opportunities* to express the Christ-life. A lifestyle ruled by law is driven by duty. This is the secret that sets people free to relax and simply enjoy life, in the power of the Holy Spirit of Christ who lives in them.

Remember Carla, whom we brought to Christ, then suffocated with rules after she trusted in Christ? Our approach was a description of the typical approach in many churches. Before people trust Christ, we tell them, "It's all Jesus. It's all Him. This isn't about you. It's *all* Him!" Then as soon as they trust Christ, we begin to teach, "Now it's up to *you*. It's about what *you* do for Him." Before they experience salvation we affirm "It's faith. Faith! Faith!" Then the moment they start to follow Jesus, we stress, "It is works. Works! Works!" What a contradiction! Paul said, "As you have received Christ Jesus the Lord, *so walk in Him*" (Colossians 2:6). The Bible teaches that we are to walk in the same way we first experienced the reality of His life—through appropriating His grace by faith!

A legalistic methodology in discipleship stems from the foundation of fear. It is the fear that people won't actually live a godly life apart from the coercive or persuasive pressure normally associated with religious indoctrination. Yet genuine grace will motivate a person to live a godly lifestyle more than a thousand laws could ever do. A legalist greatly underestimates the power of the indwelling Holy Spirit. When we know that we are free from the law, God's indwelling Spirit will cause us to awaken to the desire to serve based on our relationship to Jesus, not because of external demands to perform. Even in the ancient days of Ezekiel, God held forth the promise of the day of grace in which we live. Speaking through the prophet, he said,

> Moreover, I will give you a new heart and put a new spirit within you; and I will remove the heart of stone from your flesh and give you a heart of flesh. I will put My Spirit within you and cause you to walk in My statutes, and you will be careful to observe My ordinances (Ezekiel 36:26-27).

Millennia ago, God knew what He was going to one day do through grace. Ezekiel predicted a day when God would give us a new heart and a new spirit. He anticipated the time when we would experience an intrinsic motivation to serve God. Our wants would change! No longer would those who trusted Him respond to His commands from a sense of duty. Believers would be motivated by desire. They would no longer *struggle* to live a godly lifestyle, trying to suppress evil desires and squelch wrong behavior.

Instead, the Spirit of God would come into us and *cause* those who trust Him to carefully observe His commandments by simply resting in His empowering presence and doing what we want—because to do what we want would be to do what *He* wants! Ezekiel predicted that in this new day those who followed God would no longer act on the basis of the application of *external laws*, but rather would act out of the acceptance of the *internal life* they possessed.

We are now living in that day! To walk in grace is to know this secret and to be motivated by it. Such a person is somebody who actively serves and obeys God because he can't help it! Go ahead and try to stop him. It can't be done. He is a man on a mission, and his mission is empowered by the omnipotent God of the universe, who has taken up residence within him. Don't try telling a person walking in grace what she *must* do. She will tell you to keep your rules because she doesn't need them. She isn't doing what she's supposed to do. She is doing what she *wants* to do. The source of her behavior isn't some religious prescription; it is a real Person living within her, energizing and empowering her with divine life at every moment!

Not Knowing Our True Desires Will Defeat Us

My self-imposed family-devotional rule stole my victory in that area of my life. Of course, as I pointed out, there is nothing wrong with a man leading his family in a devotional time together. However, when I placed myself under the *law* that insisted on strict observance to the "family altar" rule, that very law incited me to disobedience. That is the nature of religious rules. They always stir us up to do the exact opposite of what they demand.

Tell yourself you cannot do something, and it stirs up passion to disobey. Paul described this perfectly in Romans 7:5: "While we were in the flesh, the sinful passions, which were *aroused* by the Law, were at work in the members of our body to bear fruit for death." The passion to rebel is aroused by the law.

In the book *The Pilgrim's Progress,* there is an incident where Christian goes into a great room that represents the human heart. The room is filled with dust, which represents sin. He takes a large broom (law) and attempts to sweep out all the dust. But instead of sweeping away the dust, he simply stirs it up into a choking cloud. That is the exact effect that law will have any time we attempt to use it as a means to eradicate sin.

What About the New Testament's Commandments?

Since trying to force ourselves to "do right" based on rules actually stimulates us to sin, what are we to do with the commandments of the New Testament? Didn't Jesus say that if we love Him, we would keep His commandments? (See John 14:15.) He did indeed. Yet when a person learns to live from the core desires that come from Christ, he or she will approach the commandments of the New Testament with a totally different attitude than the legalist. Legalism presents the commandments as divine ultimatums coming from a harsh Judge. If your perspective is that you must force yourself to do the right thing, you hear the tone of Jesus' words like this: "If you love Me, you had better keep My commandments."

We sometimes hear well-meaning Bible teachers tell us that the only commandment we have under grace is the one repeated by Jesus in Matthew 22: "You shall love the Lord your God with all your heart, and with all your soul, and with all your mind." Is this the New-Covenant law for believers? No, it isn't. We need to consider Jesus' words in their context.

One time some Pharisees (the legalists of His day) came to Jesus:

> One of them, a lawyer, asked Him a question, testing Him, "Teacher, which is the great commandment in the Law?" And He said to him, "'You shall love the Lord your God with all your heart, and with all your soul, and with all your mind.' This is the great and foremost commandment. The second is like it, 'You shall love your neighbor as yourself.' On these two commandments depend the whole Law and the Prophets."

Look at the question asked of Jesus: "Which is the great commandment *in the Law*?" What was the answer Jesus gave? "You shall love the Lord." The reason, then, why I insist that to teach we must love the Lord is legalistic is because Jesus Himself said it is the "foremost commandment" of the Law.

What does the Law do in a person's life? Paul said in Romans 7:5 that it arouses "sinful passions." In other words, it provokes the opposite response from what it tells us to do. He gives an example by pointing out that coveting wasn't a problem for him until he learned that the Law says, "Don't covet." Suddenly, he found himself coveting like crazy. (Read it for yourself in Romans 7:7-8).

The Law works like reverse psychology. It motivates you to do the exact opposite of what it tells you. So what happens to people when they are told they *should* (there's the definitive word) love God? Just the opposite arises within them. That's why so many Christians are literally praying for God to help them love Him more. It's because they are experiencing the predictable outcome of trying to live up to the commandment "You shall love the Lord your God."

What is the answer of grace to this dilemma? It is to teach people how much the Lord their God loves *them*! First John 4:19 says, "We love because He first loved us." There's the answer. To love Him more we need only understand how much He loves us! As we grow in the understanding of His unlimited, unconditional love, our response will be to love Him!

The grace walk causes a person to face the commandments with eager anticipation, not fear and intimidation. This believer understands the words of Jesus when He said, "If you love me, you will keep my commandments." When we love Jesus, we *will* keep His commandments. Obedience is the natural response of the one who loves Jesus. We *want* to be obedient. We have already learned that without love, the only thing we have to offer is lifeless compliance. *Love* is the basis for our obedience, not laws.

John stressed the relationship between love and our obedience to God's commandments when he said, "This is the love of God, that we keep His commandments; and His commandments are not burdensome" (1 John 5:3). It's not a strain for anybody who is walking in grace to obey the commandments of God. It is a pleasure to be obedient!

I travel much in my ministry. Suppose I were to ask for your advice concerning my responsibilities to my wife when I return home from a trip. How would you respond if I asked you whether or not I *must* kiss my wife when I get back? What would you think if I were to seriously ask you what I *should* do when she greets me at the front door? You would probably assume that, because I asked a question like that, something must be wrong with our relationship. In a healthy marriage, a man wouldn't ask such a foolish question. The fact is that when I see Melanie, I kiss her. I can assure you that it isn't duty that motivates me. My love for my wife animates my actions.

Thus the commandments of the New Testament do have a place in the life of a person who has learned the secret of grace. They present a beautiful blueprint that illustrates what a lifestyle looks like when it is empowered with the divine expression of the life of Jesus. When we understand the secret of doing what we want, we approach the Bible saying, "Lord, show me all the ways that Jesus can express His life through me." Then when we come across commandments, we may exclaim with excitement, "Great! Here's a way that Christ can express His life through my lifestyle!" So the commandments are not a burden, but instead are a great blessing. This is exactly what real freedom looks like.

A New Understanding Creates New Desires

Understanding grace doesn't lead to sinful desires. It has the opposite effect—it causes our motivation toward obedience to be love and desire. There was a time before we knew our true identity when we were controlled by nothing more than self-restraint. That approach certainly won't connect us to an inner desire to live a godly lifestyle. "But now we have been released from the Law, having died to that by which we were bound, so that we serve in newness of the Spirit and not in oldness of the letter" (Romans 7:6). In this newness of the Spirit, we remind ourselves that we died to the law and are no longer obligated to religious rules.

Paul wrote, "'Everything is permissible,' but not everything is helpful. 'Everything is permissible,' but not everything builds up" (1 Corinthians 10:23 HCSB). Was Paul telling the truth about this or not? It doesn't get clearer than that statement. "Everything is permissible."

If the apostle said that in a local congregation in the twenty-first century, he would probably get the same negative response he received when he taught pure grace in the early church world. When interpreted through a legalistic filter, this kind of freedom doesn't seem like it could possibly be true. What opponents of this freedom fail to understand is the transformation in heart desires that grace brings. Finally we are free to serve God because we *want* to, not because we have to. We can do what we want to do because what we want to do is caused by His empowering, motivating, course-changing, God-honoring lifestyle within us.

What's the alternative? Living by the "ought-to's"? How has that worked for you thus far? We've already seen that taking such a legalistic approach is a death sentence when it comes to living a godly lifestyle.

"Ought to" is the ammunition for the spirit of legalism. It will kill your joy every time it hits you. Are you spending your life trying to avoid doing the wrong things? Then you are living right where the enemy of your soul wants you to be. The power of the law to arouse sinful behavior is greatly underestimated by those who think self-restraint is the answer.

Imagine a woman telling her spouse, "Honey, I really *want* to have an affair, but I won't. The opportunity is there every day but *I am trying my best not to give in.* I know I shouldn't, so I won't. I'm asking God to help me to keep saying no. With His help I won't do it, even though *I really want to commit adultery.*"

Can you imagine what kind of marriage relationship that would be? The obvious question to consider is, how would our relationship to God be any different? Does it honor Him when we clench our religious jaw muscles and determine that we'll do the right thing no matter how much we really want to do just the opposite? Does that sound like something that would please Him any more than it would please a mate in marriage?

The secret to doing what we want is to recognize the wants that come from our core—where Christ makes His home. I hope you've seen in this chapter that religious rules carried out by self-discipline aren't going to change those desires. The only thing that will awaken us to desires generated by Him is to discover our true selves—people who are defined by our union with God through Jesus in the Spirit. When we know that, we can do what we want with confidence that the desires we experience have their source in the One in whom we find our authentic selves.

❧ WALKING TOGETHER

Dear Father,

I acknowledge that I have often fallen victim to foolish behavior because I've relied on self-restraint instead of Spirit-generated desires. The personal struggle to avoid wrong and do good has seemed so right to me. I see now that an approach like that is the essence of a works system, and that's not the way You have designed me to live. Now I realize I will never experience Your life through sheer determination to do right. I have made the mistake of trying to move forward spiritually by my own works. I have trusted in my own self-discipline and not in the sufficiency of Your Life within me. Right now I affirm that You are my victory. Teach me to trust You and to be motivated by Your desires, not a sense

*of religious duty. Awaken me to the wants You have
placed in me. I love You, Lord Jesus. May that be my
motivation in life.*

✤ GROUP QUESTIONS

1. What is the problem with suppressing wrong desires
   and trying to do the right thing, as opposed to learning
   how to live from desires given to us by God? Read
   Romans 7:5 and describe how laws affect us. Discuss
   an example from your own life that illustrates how you
   set yourself up for failure by embracing a religious rule
   and determining to enforce it in your own lifestyle.

2. Why did God give the Law even when He knew man
   would not keep it? Did keeping the Law save people in
   the Old Testament? What purpose does the Law serve
   today in the life of a believer? Of an unbeliever? What
   Bible verses substantiate your answers?

3. How would you describe legalistic discipleship? What
   are the elements of discipleship that are grounded
   in grace? How does proper discipleship help people
   connect to the God-given desires within them?

4. What would you say to the person who expresses fear
   that teaching grace may encourage people to go wild
   with sinning? How would you answer the person
   who says, "I don't have to pray, read my Bible, or do
   anything else since I'm under grace"?

5. Read Ezekiel 36:26-27. What does this verse mean
   when it speaks about our receiving a new spirit?
   How does God cause us to walk in His statutes? Do
   we play any part in this process? If so, what is our
   responsibility?

6. How do rules steal our victory? What rules can you
   identify that have robbed you of your victory? Were

you taught certain rules as soon as you were saved? What are they?

7. What place do New Testament commandments have in our lives today? How do you interpret John 14:15? Discuss the difference between a legalistic understanding of this verse and an understanding based on grace.

Chapter 6

THE SECRET OF THE RIGHT FOCUS

When I was a boy I loved to play marbles. I would often go out into the backyard and draw a circle in the dirt, put a handful of marbles "in the pot," and shoot marbles for hours. I often played with my friends, with each of us putting ten marbles in the circle and taking turns shooting. Did I play for keeps? Well, I'll just say that I had a *big* bag of marbles! I couldn't imagine a day ever coming when I would give up that hobby. I knew that one day I would grow old enough that I would look pretty silly on the ground with my favorite shooter, but I tried not to think about those days. I wanted to play forever.

One day while I was outside practicing, I heard someone call my name. I looked over toward the backyard of my friend Phillip and saw him there with Ricky and Danny. They were standing under a basketball hoop that hadn't been there the day before. "We're gonna play a game. We need a fourth man. Want to play?" they asked. I left my marbles in the dirt that day and never looked back. I had found a new passion.

I loved to play basketball. Every single day I couldn't wait to get home from school so I could rush out into the backyard to play ball. Every day we would play until dark. Fridays were especially exciting—because we didn't have school the next day, our parents would often allow us to stay outside very late, shooting baskets when we could hardly even see the hoop. It was an adolescent boy's paradise.

Now this is something I can do all my life! I reasoned. *Mr. Lambert across the street still plays basketball and he's a grown man!* In those days I was convinced that there would never be a Friday night of my life when I didn't shoot basketball. I was addicted to it.

One Sunday when I was barely 16 years old our family went to church. While sitting in the Sunday school class that morning, I noticed a new girl who walked into the class. I had never seen her before. I had never been on a date up to that time. When this girl walked past me, I checked her out—I mean, I *discerned* that this might be a good time to begin my dating life.

I went home and asked my dad the big question. "Dad, if I get a date some Friday night, will you let me use your car to go out?" "Do you have a date?" my dad asked, probably glad to see his only son moving toward manhood. "Not yet," I answered. "But there's a girl I want to go out with if you'll let me use the car." "Who is she?" he asked. "A girl I met at church last week," I said. "Okay," he replied. "You can use the car if you get a date."

I couldn't wait until the next Sunday. As soon as church was over I made a beeline for this new girl. After some nervous small talk, I took the plunge. "Are you doing anything this Friday night?" I asked. "No," she answered, "why?" "Well, there's a new Barbra Streisand movie coming out this weekend. I thought we could go see it and then go over to Pizza Villa after the movie, if you want to," I said. "Sure, that sounds like fun," she replied.

The following Friday night I picked her up and went out on my first date. It went very well. The next day my buddies all rushed over to my house bright and early. "Where were you?"

they demanded. "We waited for you to come out. We play basketball *every* Friday!" they exclaimed with obvious irritation over my reckless disregard for our sacred routine. "Why didn't you join us?" Holding my shoulders back with my head held high, I answered, "Boys, I had a date!"

To their dismay, I called the girl and asked her to go out with me the following Friday. She accepted. In fact, I went out with her every Friday for the next three years, and then I married her. We've been married since 1973. Now that I think about it, I can't remember the last time I played basketball on a Friday night. I had found something better!

We Don't Overcome Sin by Focusing on It

When you find yourself entangled with a sin, it is often hard to imagine a time when you won't be connected to that sin. How do you find freedom over habitual sins? Certainly it won't happen by applying religious rules to your life. We have already seen how trying to fight temptation with sheer willpower arouses a person's desire to sin. The idea that you should protect yourself from sin by strict adherence to rules through the power of self-discipline is a direct route to failure. Religious rules *always* stimulate sin.

I hate to compare wholesome activities like marbles and basketball to sin, but I want to use my experience with these as an analogy. If somebody had told me when I was a young child that I would *have* to give up marbles, I would have resisted the idea. If someone had suggested that at age 16 I would be required to give up Friday-night basketball, I would have rebelled against the very thought. As it was, I didn't focus on giving up either. I simply became obsessed with something else I wanted more than those things—to be more accurate, *someone* else. One might say that Melanie delivered me from basketball. It wasn't a struggle for me; I just set my mind on her and basketball sort of faded away.

This is exactly how the secret to the right focus works in your grace walk. When we come to know what this union we share with Jesus means and focus on Him, we discover that sins we once couldn't imagine living without lose their appeal to us. We don't experience victory by struggling against sins, but by setting our attention on Jesus. The apostle Paul said it succinctly in Colossians 3:1-3:

> If you have been raised up with Christ, keep seeking the things above, where Christ is, seated at the right hand of God. Set your mind on the things above, not on the things that are on earth. For you have died and your life is hidden with Christ in God.

We will never overcome sin through sheer determination and self-discipline. Don't stare at the thing you hate! That kind of negative motivation keeps our eyes off Jesus and on our sins. We are to focus on Him, not sin! As we fall more and more in love with Him, those sins that we have so tightly clung to will become increasingly unattractive to us—until we *want* to let them go.

When I was a child, we sometimes sang an old song that clearly teaches God's method for overcoming sin. It says, "Turn your eyes upon Jesus, look full in His wonderful face, and the things of earth will grow strangely dim in the light of His glory and grace." The repellent for sin is not self-effort. The remedy will always be nothing other than Jesus.

Reaping What We Sow

To think that focusing on overcoming our sins will give us the freedom we want is a totally wrong approach to the matter. Not only will setting our mind on fleshly failures not bring victory, it will actually perpetuate our defeat. A legalistic approach will always cause us to focus on behavior, but when we come to understand the secret of the right focus, we stop starting in the wrong place and put our attention where it belongs.

Those who are according to the flesh set their minds
on the things of the flesh, but those who are according to the Spirit, the things of the Spirit. For the
mind set on the flesh is death, but the mind set on
the Spirit is life and peace (Romans 8:5-6).

Paul asserts that whatever you set your mind on will ultimately determine your behavior. If a man continually sets his
mind on bass fishing, it will only be a matter of time before he is
trying to figure out how to buy a bass boat. Those who set their
minds on football usually can be found in front of the television
on weekends and holidays, watching football—or playing the
game on a field with some friends.

If we set our mind on sinning, we should not be surprised
when our behavior matches our mindset. We guarantee our
own failure when we decide to overcome sin by concentrat-
ing on it. It will make no difference that we ask God to help us.
God won't bless our efforts to deliver ourselves from sin after
we have trusted Him any more than He would help us overcome sin before we believed on Him. He wants us to realize that
our attempts to achieve victory over sin are futile—so that we
will focus our attention on Jesus. As long as we try to gain victory through our behavior, God will patiently wait until we have
exhausted all our options. Then He will do for us what we can't
do for ourselves. It is at that point that we are ready to receive
His answer.

Lies That Bind

If you keep on focusing on the things you don't want to do,
you already know what is going to happen. So how do we change
our focus? The first step in knowing how to change focus from
our sins to Jesus is to understand our real attitude toward sin.
Many believers who find themselves enslaved to a particular sin
operate under the mistaken belief that they love that sin. They
assume there is no way to be free from something they love.

"I hate myself!" Those were the first words Jim spoke after our initial introduction to each other. He had scheduled an appointment with me to discuss "a personal problem." "Why do you hate yourself?" I asked him. As Jim began to explain his problem to me, I learned that he was addicted to pornography.

"I can't help myself," he said. "I have come to love pornographic videos. I tell myself I won't watch them anymore, but like clockwork I find myself back online browsing porn sites. I'm disgusted with myself!"

Jim was a victim of the same lie that keeps many in bondage to sin. He confessed that he hated himself and loved the sin. In reality, Jim didn't even know himself. And he certainly didn't love the sin that had brought him to see me after he had gotten to the place of absolute desperation. In the weeks ahead, I was able to share with him some truths that helped to set him free.

Jesus said, "You will know the truth, and the truth will make you free" (John 8:32). God's truth always sets people free when they come to know it, especially considering the fact that the "truth" isn't a principle but Jesus Himself. The corollary to this statement is that if knowing truth sets a person free, believing lies binds a person. So to the extent that anybody experiences bondage, he or she believes a lie. But when that person knows the truth, he or she discovers freedom.

Sin Is Repulsive to the Christian

Jim believed he loved his secret sin. In reality, he didn't love it at all. He hated it. He had made the mistake of thinking he loved his sin just because he kept indulging in it. If he had genuinely loved the sin, he never would have come to my office seeking help. He would have been perfectly content to continue in it. The reason for his emotional misery was because he was enslaved to a sin he hated.

The apostle Paul described his own encounter with sin,

saying, "What I am doing, I do not understand; for I am not practicing what I would like to do, but I am doing the very thing I hate…For the good that I wish, I do not do, but I practice the very evil that I do not want" (Romans 7:15,19).

Paul honestly confessed that he sinned. I'm glad he was honest about it. Don't ever think that you are the only one who has struggled with personal sins. The man who wrote most of the books in the New Testament openly admitted that he had seen days of great struggles with sin.

Paul affirmed that although he did sin, nothing in him loved it. The description of his attitude is given in Romans 7:15-25. After describing his struggle, he declares in verse 24: "Wretched man that I am! Who will set me free from the body of this death?" The word "wretched" means miserable. That will eventually be the experience of everybody who struggles with sin. We weren't made to live that way, and we won't know peace when we do.

Is there sin in your own life that comes to mind as you read these words? It is important for you to see your real attitude toward it in order to be set free from its power. Don't be deceived into believing you love sin just because you find yourself going back to it and finding it pleasurable. You were created to live in the loving embrace of Righteousness personified. Sin can never satisfy you. That's why you know deep within that something just doesn't fit when you live that way.

The Bible teaches that sin brings pleasure for a while but eventually things turn sour. Some people don't understand that it is possible to enjoy sin and hate it at the same time. If you didn't hate your sin, you wouldn't find yourself struggling with it or even caring about it. The fact that you may enjoy it says nothing about you, but simply demonstrates something about the nature of sin—that it can be pleasurable. Jim failed to understand this fact and had embraced the lie that he loved pornography.

Sin Doesn't Define You

Jim's declaration "I hate myself" reveals another lie he believed—a lie that kept him enslaved. He identified himself by the sin that held him. He believed that pornography was a part of who he was as a man. He made no distinction whatsoever between his actions and his identity. Consequently, he saw himself as his own worst enemy.

His misunderstanding is common among those who fail to understand their identity in Christ. Until you know who you are, your perception of yourself will fuel bad behavior and reinforce an unreal understanding of your authentic entity. To commit sin stands in stark contradiction to your identity founded in Christ Himself. It is a total contradiction of who Jesus Christ has made you to become through His atonement.

In describing his own sinful behavior, Paul made two points clear. First, he expressed how much he hated his sin. Then he made a definite distinction between his true self and the seductive power of sin he sensed. Twice he asserted that when he sinned, it was no longer he who sinned, "but sin which dwells in me" (Romans 7:17,20).

When Paul said that, was he trying to shirk responsibility for his sin? Was he suggesting, as some people do, "The devil made me do it"? Absolutely not. Paul accepted full responsibility for the choices he made. He was simply clarifying that when we sin, it is a contradiction of our own nature. In his statements about sin, he revealed that there was a power of enticement he experienced within him *that was not him.* Paul wasn't evil, but he was still capable of hearing seducing lies that could entice him toward evil unless he found his protection in Christ's strength and not his own. It's easy to live under an assumed identity that deceives us when we don't know what Christ has done, not only *for* us, but also *to* us.

There is a power that pulls us toward sinful actions, but that power is not who we are. It's not part of us. It is a lie that comes in to distract our focus from the Truth that empowers us to live the life we were made for by our God. This fact must be recognized if we want to experience victory.

Many of us have wrongly believed that there is an evil person living inside us. We have a great desire to glorify God, yet we see what we wrongly believe to be "another side of us." That's not you. I used to feel like I had an "evil twin" living within me who wanted to have control of my lifestyle. Consequently, I often prayed for God to help me so the part of me that was evil would be subdued. I worked hard to suppress what I believed to be the evil part of me. Paul, however, distanced himself from this enticement to do wrong:

> If I do the very thing I do not wish to do, I agree with the Law, confessing that the Law is good. So now, no longer am I the one doing it, but sin which dwells in me. For I know that nothing good dwells in me, that is, in my flesh; for the willing is present in me, but the doing of the good is not. For the good that I want, I do not do; but I practice the very evil that I do not want. But if I am doing the very thing I do not want, I am no longer the one doing it, but sin which dwells in me (Romans 7:16-20).

Does this sound like the confession of an evil man? Does it sound like a man who loves sin? Paul said he was doing the thing that he did not want to do. He said that the wishing to do good was always present in him, despite the fact that his actions might at times indicate otherwise. Does this predicament resemble your own experience? You may have assumed you are a bad person simply because you recognize something internally seducing you toward sin at times. That inclination you sense, however, is not you! Paul continues:

> I find then the principle that evil is present in me, the one who wants to do good. For I joyfully concur with

the law of God in the inner man, but I see a different
law in the members of my body, waging war against
the law of my mind, and making me a prisoner of the
law of sin which is in my members (7:21-23).

What a discovery to realize that you are not evil! Paul
described our situation perfectly, saying, "I find then the principle that evil *is present in me*, the one who wishes to do good."
He recognized the distinction between the power of sin and his
own identity. He did not see himself as an evil man, but recognized that evil enticed him from within. If you put your focus
in the wrong place, you can be defeated by whispered lies about
who you *aren't* and what you *don't want* to do but momentarily
may think you want to.

The Key to Victory

We take an essential step toward victory when we understand
we are not our own enemy. The enemy is the power of sin. I'm
not suggesting that through Christ we haven't been delivered
from sin's power. It's simply a matter of learning not to define
ourselves by the inner temptations we still sometimes sense.
Once we make the distinction between internal enticements to
do wrong and our authentic selves, then we are in a position to
take the next step toward the lifestyle we are equipped to know
and enjoy. This step involves answering an important question
raised by the apostle Paul.

Paul presents the definitive question regarding sin in
Romans 7:24 when he asks, "Who will set me free from the body
of this death?" Overcoming our sin involves asking the right
question. For 29 years after I became a Christian, I asked all the
wrong questions. The wrong questions will never lead to a right
answer! Concerning my sins, I sometimes asked, "*What* can I
do to experience victory?" At other times, I prayed, "Lord, *how*
can I overcome my sins?" Paul didn't ask such questions. He

recognized that the key to victory doesn't come by asking *what* or *how*. The key to victory over sin is a *Who*! Asking *what* or *how* suggests that we believe there must be a plan or method that can enable us to overcome sin. God's provision for our sins is not a plan, but the Person of Jesus Christ.

Soaring with Jesus

The principle of indwelling sin is a reality Paul faced and you will face. Yes, the work of Christ is finished, yet we have discovered that sin is still a force with which we must reckon. However, God has given us the antidote for the power of sin through Jesus Christ. After his lengthy discourse on the problem in Romans 7, Paul sets forth this truth with clarity in chapter 8, verse 2: "The law of the Spirit of life in Christ Jesus has set you free from the law of sin and of death."

The law of sin and death is always present, seeking to pull us down into independent living at every moment, but there is another law in which we may rest. It is the law of the Spirit of life in Christ Jesus. The latter law will always supersede the former. As we trust Him, Jesus will never fail to overcome the law of sin and death.

Imagine that you were told a woman jumped off the Empire State Building in New York City. What image comes to your mind? You may ask many questions about that incident, but one thing you would never ask is, "Did she fall?" You would assume she fell because of your understanding of the law of gravity. It is a universal law that affects everybody.

What if you then were told that the woman who jumped had been holding onto a hang glider? Your mental picture immediately changes because of your understanding of another law—the law of aerodynamics. With the added information, you wouldn't envision her falling; instead you would see her soaring over the skyline of New York. While you recognize the law of gravity, you also understand that, in a situation like this, the law of aerodynamics would overcome the law of gravity.

Does the law of gravity cease to exist while the woman is soaring with the hang glider? Not at all, but she is resting in a higher law. That's how it works in your life. While the power of sin is real, the law of sin and death is not able to find its expression as long as a person rests in the sufficiency of Christ. There is an Eternal Reality that stands above the experiential reality you may know. At every moment that we depend totally on Him to express His life through us, we will experience victory over sin.

When you are flying in an airplane, are you focused on falling or flying? I suspect you relax, sit back, and live in the awareness of the reliability of the plane and the competency of the pilot. Otherwise, you certainly don't enjoy flying. That's the way it is in life. Christ has done what He has done on your behalf, but the trip surely will be much more enjoyable if you learn to relax and trust Him. It's the secret of the right focus.

What would happen if the woman with the hang glider decided that she wanted to function independently of it? At the exact moment she decided to do so, the law of gravity would once again become operative and she would immediately fall. If she chose to separate herself from the hang glider, nobody would be surprised that she fell. In fact, they wouldn't expect anything else.

When we rest in Christ, depending on Him as our life source at every moment, we will experience victory over sin. However, at any moment we decide to function apart from Jesus, we will sin. The sin won't be the wrong act itself, but rather the independent attitude that precipitated the wrong deed.

There is no other possibility if we don't trust Christ. There is no middle ground. Either we choose to depend entirely on Him or else we don't. When our focus is on Him, victory is the natural expression of His life within us. We soar above the downward pull of indwelling sin because we are carried along by the gentle breeze of His love.

We will never be free from the presence of sin as long as we live in the physical bodies we now possess. But when this secret of the right focus governs your thoughts, you will find freedom from the power of sin. God, of course, will allow us to play in the dirt with our sins if that is what we choose to do. However, I want to encourage you to look up from your sins and check out the One beside you. When you see His glorious beauty and hear His enrapturing voice, don't be surprised if you find yourself wanting to leave your sins and go follow Him. After that, why would you ever want to look anyplace else?

WALKING TOGETHER

Dear Father,

You know all the sins in my life. Thank You for showing me that I hate those sins, even when I have found pleasure in them. I acknowledge that my sins don't reflect who I truly am. From this point forward, I choose to set my focus on You, not my sins. Lord Jesus, I can't deliver myself from my own bad behavior. I trust You to cause me to experience victory over sin's power. May I learn to receive Your love so I may be so caught up in You that my sins simply fall away. I trust You to enable me to experience the freedom You provide.

GROUP QUESTIONS

1. Read Colossians 3:1-3. How does setting our focus on Christ enable us to find freedom over sin's power? Discuss how this passage relates to what Paul had to say in Romans 8 about setting our mind on the things of the flesh.

2. What were the two lies Jim believed that kept him enslaved to pornography? List some other common lies the enemy uses to keep us from experiencing freedom over sins. Identify a specific lie you have believed about your own sins.

3. Discuss the meaning of *indwelling sin*. What verses prove that the power of sin is not a part of your identity? Paraphrase Romans 7:16-20 in your own words.

4. What are some common methods people try in an effort to overcome personal sins? Explain the meaning of Romans 7:24-25.

5. What is the law of sin and death? What is the law of the Spirit of life in Christ Jesus? How do we experience the law of the Spirit of life in Christ Jesus?

6. How would you relate to a friend who is living in open sin? What would you say to this person? What verses would you show him or her?

Chapter 7

THE SECRET OF CAREFREE LIVING

"Pray for me to know God's will," Brent said. "I have three job offers and I'm not sure which one I'm supposed to accept. I don't want to miss God's perfect will by taking a job I'm not supposed to have," he continued. "Please pray that the right choice will become very clear to me *soon*."

Brent was a close friend of mine, and I knew he had a sincere desire to honor God in the decisions he made in his life. Yet I could see he was experiencing real anxiety over which choice to make in this matter. He had been without a job for almost three months, but now he had three offers, all coming within days of each other. The irony of the situation was that he had seemed more relaxed during the months he had had no job offers than he did now when he had three. Any of the three sounded good to me, but his concern over picking the right option made him tense.

Brent needed to understand the secret of carefree living. That may sound impossible, but when you confidently come to rest in the reality of the goodness of God, your perspective changes on everything. You begin to understand that every detail of life flows from your relationship with One who will *ensure* that your steps are the right ones.

Grace means that God does it all. Do you believe that? "But don't we have a part?" you may ask. We have one "part"—we simply receive from Him, cooperating with the Holy Spirit by trusting Him moment by moment. To walk in grace doesn't mean we are passive in matters of daily living. To the contrary, it means that we act in confidence, resting in the fact that it is God who will initiate, perpetuate, and consummate His plan for our lives.

So many people fall short of the joy God intends for them because they fail to understand how His grace acts on our behalf to bring to pass the wonderful plan He has for us. If it really is true that my life is completely in His hands and that He is the One who is responsible for seeing that I fulfill the plan He has for me, then I can relax! I can dance my way through a carefree life, not acting irresponsibly but, to the contrary, acting *boldly* in the knowledge that my Loving Father ultimately is the force behind all that happens to me.

God has an awesome plan for your life. It isn't a cookie-cutter plan, either. He designed a special agenda, an agenda uniquely created for you. Before you were ever born, He saw you and customized His plan for your lifetime. One of the greatest joys in life is to know that you are experiencing the very purpose for which you were created. Fulfilling the will of God is not some elusive goal that can never be reached. It is possible to enjoy the experience of *knowing* we are in the very center of God's purpose.

Changing Our Perspective

Do you want to experience the joy of carefree living? Then it is important to understand the difference between a legalistic approach to life and resting in Him through the grace walk. A legalistic mindset sees life as all about *doing*. It produces the belief that it is our responsibility to find and fulfill God's specific plan for our lives. Believers caught up in this lie are often sincere, yet their perspective actually cheats them out of the greatest benefit associated with living the lifestyle God has designed for them. The greatest blessing in experiencing God's will is the joy of experiencing God Himself! Yet legalists are so focused on making the right choice that they usually miss the carefree abandon God intends that they enjoy. They believe they have a job to do for God. Because of their drive to *do something*, they often make better church members than Christians. They *can* often accomplish many good things. The only problem with the things they do is that God is nowhere to be found in their activity. That is a serious problem.

God's Plan for You Is Jesus

The starting point for understanding God's plan for your life must be grace. Remember that legalism is the method of living in which we try to make spiritual progress based on what we do. A legalistic mind asks, "*What* is the will of God for me? What should I do?" Yet before we can correctly relate to the *what* of God's will, we must properly relate to the *Who* of His will. The will of God is not first and foremost a plan, but instead is a Person. Jesus Christ is the will of God. When we rightly relate to Him, effortlessly fulfilling the plan He has becomes the natural result of the union shared with Him.

Many people, including no small number of Christians, live like Deists. A Deist basically believes that God created the world, fueled it up like a car, and then stepped back to watch it run its course. Deism recognizes very little personal interaction between the Creator and His creation. Its perspective could be pictured this way: God has empowered the car (earth) to run, and now it is up to mankind where he drives it. Of course, those who understand the biblical witness to our Father would contest such a view. We believe He is very much involved in the detailed events of this world. Yet many people act like Deists when it comes to God's will for their own lives. They look for Him to show them His will so they can learn their assignment and then go out and do it. They fail to see the cooperative partnership they can experience by realizing that there is no assignment. Life is a dance, and our Dance Partner simply leads us in the steps in synch with the rhythms of His love.

In his book *Experiencing God,* Henry Blackaby uses a great illustration to demonstrate how God purposes to accomplish His will within us. He suggests there are two ways a person can reach a destination to which he has never been. He or she can ask directions from a friend who has been there. That friend can draw a map that clearly shows how to reach the destination. That method may work, assuming the driver knows how to read a map and then reads and follows it correctly. However, there is a second way that would absolutely guarantee that the driver would reach the desired destination. Instead of asking for a map, he or she could ask the friend to join the trip and point out the way as they drove. In that way the friend would *become* the map.

That's a perfect description of how Jesus wants us to live our lives. When we understand our union with Him, He *becomes* the will of God to us, expressing His life through us so every detail of God's will is fulfilled in our lifestyles. Jesus is the One who can cause us to know and do the will of God. Apart from Him, there is no way we can experience the will of the Father. Paul said, "It is God who is at work in you, both to will and to work for His good pleasure" (Philippians 2:13). God the Holy Spirit within us will fulfill the Father's plan as we are absorbed into a continuous awareness of our oneness with Christ. To be more accurate with the illustration, Jesus isn't just our map—He is the driver, the car, and the road. He is everything to us!

What Are You Seeking?

The goal of wanting to know God's will is a noble one if properly understood. A clear understanding will draw a person toward Jesus Christ. When we understand the secret of carefree living, we can simply walk by faith with Jesus in the full knowledge that He is guiding our steps toward the purposes God intends for us to fulfill. This knowledge is so liberating because it's not up to us to make something happen! It really is all up to Him, and He will do it.

Our inclination toward seeking the right path places the responsibility on us to figure out God's will. When we walk in a faith-filled, carefree lifestyle, we understand that humanity is the recipient of good things and God is the Giver. So under grace, it isn't our job to *find* God's will, but rather to rest in the confidence that He will *reveal* His will to us. A person trapped in a legalistic mindset will pursue God's will with sincerity and yet never be confident that he or she has discovered it—and will never know what carefree living can be. One who enjoys a calm confidence in Jesus will know it without struggling to find it.

A biblical model for knowing the will of God is presented in Acts 13, where Paul and Barnabas were sent out on a missionary journey by the church at Antioch. How did this church know whom to send out as their very first missionaries? There was no missions committee meeting in which key leaders decided that the church needed to begin a missions program. How did these early Christians know the will of God concerning the great missionary Paul? Luke records how it happened:

> Now there were at Antioch, in the church that was there, prophets and teachers: Barnabas, and Simeon who was called Niger, and Lucius of Cyrene, and Manaen who had been brought up with Herod the tetrarch, and Saul. While they were ministering to the Lord and fasting, the Holy Spirit said, "Set apart

> for Me Barnabas and Saul for the work to which I
> have called them." Then, when they had fasted and
> prayed and laid their hands on them, they sent them
> away (Acts 13:1-3).

The key to their understanding of God's will is that it was revealed to them "while they were ministering to the Lord and fasting." These early church members weren't simply seeking to know the *will* of God; they were seeking *God*, and He spoke clearly to them, making His will clearly known. They discovered the *plan* while they were seeking the *Person* of God.

While legalism insists that we find the will of God, God's grace enables us to know His will as we personally experience Him. Legalism puts the burden on the individual to listen hard enough to hear God's will. The secret of carefree living accompanies the understanding that He is capable of making His plans known to us!

Imagine a dad coming into the room where his teenage son is watching television. "I want you to cut the grass," he might say. The son doesn't respond. The program he is watching has mesmerized him.

"Did you hear me? I want you to cut the grass," the dad repeats. Still no response.

"Son!" the father says louder.

"Yes, sir?" the boy finally answers.

"I want you to cut the grass."

"Okay, Dad."

Is the man angry with his son because he honestly didn't hear? Of course not. The man wouldn't scold him, saying, "Whenever you are watching television, you had better keep one ear open to me in case I want something from you!" He would know that, in that instance, the burden of communication is on him.

That's how it is with God. He is our heavenly Father, and it is

His responsibility to cause us to hear when He speaks. You don't have to be filled with care and concern about missing God's will because you weren't listening carefully enough. As you simply trust in Christ, He assumes the responsibility of causing you to hear.

What are you seeking? What good would it do somebody to discover the plan God had for him if he were not fully aware of His union with Jesus Christ? By what power can we fulfill His purpose apart from Him? Given numerous options, does it matter which one we choose if we then seek to carry out the plan by our own strengths and abilities? Even if we knew the right plan, it would be pointless to seek to do God's will apart from intimate dependence upon Him. When we live in total dependence upon Him, His will most certainly will be revealed with absolutely no concerns on our part. That's how to experience God's will through grace!

Cooperating with the Spirit

While it is God's responsibility to work out the details of our lives and not ours to figure it out on our own, that doesn't mean we are oblivious to the process by which He makes His will known. Don't misinterpret the fact that we are free from struggling to know God's will to mean that we are passive in the process. The Bible clearly teaches how we may cooperate with God in such a way as to expedite the revelation of His plans for us. There is a way to *prove* the will of God in our lives.

> I urge you, brethren, by the mercies of God, to present your bodies a living and holy sacrifice, acceptable to God, which is your spiritual service of worship. And do not be conformed to this world, but be transformed by the renewing of your mind, so that you may prove what the will of God is, that which is good and acceptable and perfect (Romans 12:1-3).

The apostle Paul suggests that there is a way to prove the will of God in our lives. It isn't necessary for us to wander through life filled with cares and concerns about whether or not we are in God's will. Our cooperation with the Holy Spirit will guarantee that we find His will in a way that proves to be "good and acceptable and perfect."

Being a Living Sacrifice

Paul indicates that our first response to God in discovering His will is to yield ourselves to Him as a "living and holy sacrifice." Every Jew in Rome who read these words knew exactly what Paul was referring to by that phrase. After Abraham's son Isaac was finally born, God told Abraham to take his only son and offer him as a sacrifice on a mountain in the land of Moriah. Genesis 22:1-14 tells the story of how Isaac was taken to the mountain, bound, and laid on an altar to be destroyed by the knife in his own father's hand. While Isaac certainly must have been frightened when he realized his father's intent, there is no evidence in the narrative that he struggled against Abraham. His dad was an old man who easily could have been overcome. Yet it appears that the son yielded to his father's will, allowing himself to be bound and laid out for the sacrifice. Only when the angel of the Lord stopped Abraham did Isaac realize he wasn't going to die.

Paul says that in order to demonstrate the will of God in our lives, we have to become like Isaac. We must totally surrender ourselves to God, yielding to His purpose regardless of what it may be. Absolute abandon to God is the foundation of knowing His will. Presenting ourselves as a living sacrifice means that we take our hands off our own lives and totally yield to Him. Absolute surrender brings an attitude of trust in Him with no conditions or strings attached. It is an affirmation that we will trust God and yield to Him, just as Isaac yielded to Abraham.

For months, Walt had lived with a nagging fear he was about

to lose his job. Rumors were circulating that his company was downsizing and that his department would suffer the most cutbacks. He had spent two months frantically looking for another job, to no avail. "I don't know what I'm going to do if I lose this job," he told me. "You know my wife is a homemaker, and we don't have much in our savings account. We will be in serious trouble if my job is phased out."

What would you tell Walt? Would you try to encourage him by assuring him that God would make certain he didn't lose his job? That would be a mistake. People sometimes find themselves unemployed. That's the world we live in today. Would you console him by telling him that he would definitely find a new job before he lost his current one? In reality, that might not happen either. Walt's need is to totally surrender his job situation to God. Right now he is holding on to the *right* to have a job. Whenever we hold on to personal rights, we set ourselves up to be tyrannized by fear when those rights are threatened. The only way to experience carefree living is to go through life with a loose grip on everything around us. *He* is the only security we have in life—and He is enough!

When we totally abandon ourselves to God, we bring ourselves to a place where we can experience the unfolding of His plan in ways we never could have imagined. It is sometimes scary to release our grip on our own lives in order to experience His life, but it is the only way to know and do His will!

I didn't encourage Walt about his employment at all. I did explain to him that the things we fear control us. I encouraged him to pray a prayer of absolute surrender to God, voluntarily giving up the right to his job. I advised him to continually acknowledge that God was his source of supply, not his employer. Only by choosing to be a living sacrifice was he able to overcome the fear that enslaved him.

In 1995, when it became apparent to our family that God was calling us out of the pastorate of a local church and into an itinerant ministry, Melanie and I faced some real fears. We had just built a new home that we were enjoying. Now God was leading us away from the apparent security of my predictable salary as a church pastor to a place where we would be required to live totally by faith, trusting Him to provide our income. Imaginary voices began to whisper in our minds about all the things that could go wrong if we followed what we believed was God's plan for us. The possibility of falling behind on our house payments and ultimately losing our home was a nagging thought for us both. Would such a step of faith prove to be our financial undoing? We were scared. Carefree living was about as far from the radar of my experience as anything could be. I cared much—too much.

Fears have a way of showing you the rights to which you're still clinging. Our fears revealed to us that we were holding on to the right to own the house we had built. We knew that the only way to be free of that fear was to completely surrender ourselves to God. So one Friday we spent the night at a nearby mountain lodge where we could be alone and face our fears. While we were there, we listed an inventory of the things we possessed in this world. We also wrote down every fear that came to our minds. We identified all the painful things that could happen as a result of our obedience to God in resigning the pastorate. Then we took our list and together prayed our way down the items we had identified. We gave up the right to stay in our house—in fact, we *gave* the house to God that night. We acknowledged every right we were holding onto that the Lord had shown us, and we relinquished those rights. The next day we left that place totally free.

Today we don't worry about losing our house. We can't lose our house now because we have already lost it. No, the mortgage company hasn't foreclosed on the property. We lost it that night on the mountain when we gave it to God. He still lets us live in it, but we don't fear losing it now because it isn't ours to lose.

Being a Holy Sacrifice

To cooperate with the Holy Spirit so we can live a carefree life requires total abandon as a *living* sacrifice. Yet Paul added that we are to present ourselves as a *holy* sacrifice too. Many generally misunderstand this aspect of surrender. The legalist believes it is his responsibility to make himself holy through disciplined devotion and religious regiment. Could anything be further from carefree living? The fact is that there is nothing a person can do to make himself holy. Nor is there a need for this, because holiness is a gift bound up in the person of Christ. Unless we understand that we have been made holy through our union with Jesus Christ, we will never enjoy the will of God, because of our focus on ourselves. We will be a slave to trying to do whatever we imagine is necessary to become a holy person.

The same single phrase in Scripture teaches that we are to be both a *living* and *holy* sacrifice. You will never hear anyone suggest that believers should try to be more alive when they present themselves to God. We all know we are totally alive already. Yet many believe they should be holier in order to present themselves to God. However, both life and holiness come from the same source—Jesus Christ! He is our life. He is our holiness. We aren't to strive for either, but simply believe His Word and receive what He has given us. Paul said,

> By His doing you are in Christ Jesus, who became to us wisdom from God, and *righteousness* and sanctification, and redemption, so that, just as it is written, "Let him who boasts, boast in the Lord" (1 Corinthians 1:30-31).

Jesus has become our righteousness; therefore, the biblical instruction to present ourselves as a holy sacrifice simply involves acknowledging who we are in Him as we yield ourselves to the Father. When you recognize that you possess the righteous nature of Jesus, you will be able to receive the revelation of God's will for you without interference from the mistaken notion that you must first improve yourself before you can be totally yielded to Him.

Doing the Will of God

"Pray for me. I have a major decision to make and I don't want to get out of God's will," Judy explained. "You know Satan is really deceptive, and I don't want to be deceived. Pray that God will protect me from a mistake. I don't want His second best. Pray that I'll make the right choice."

Although she was sincere, Judy's prayer request bordered on a worship service in Satan's honor. Her request is typical of the approach taken by many who are far too concerned about going astray in life. Notice how she expressed confidence in Satan's ability to deceive and mislead her. She was afraid she would unintentionally stumble out of God's will. She was giving far more credit to the enemy than he deserves. By contrast, when you are confident in the Father's loving oversight in your life, you will rest in the confidence that He is "able to keep you from stumbling" (Jude 24).

Understanding that Jesus Christ is God's will personified sets you free from anxiety about missing His will. If you are depending on Christ, trusting Him to animate your actions, you can move forward in faith, not fear. When Jesus Christ expresses His life through us, it is impossible to get out of the will of God! If we gave as much credit to the ability of the Holy Spirit to guide us into God's will as many give to Satan's ability to lure us out of God's will, freedom would reign!

Have you found yourself verbally expressing your faith in Satan's ability to deceive you? If so, stop it. Just relax and trust Jesus! If He is expressing His thoughts and actions through you, there is no reason for anxiety. In His grace, God gently guides us into His plans for our lives, and all of hell can't stop that!

Nobody has ever said it better than King Nebuchadnezzar. In Daniel 4:35, he confessed that God "does according to His will in the host of heaven and among the inhabitants of the earth; and no one can ward off His hand or say to Him, 'What have You done?'" *God will do whatever He wants to do!*

We don't need to agonize over the will of God. If knowing and doing His will depended on our own strength and ability, then we would have no hope. But it isn't up to us! Jesus will fight every battle to guarantee that we accomplish the will of His Father. Four hundred years ago, Martin Luther rightly wrote,

> Did we in our own strength confide,
> our striving would be losing,
> Were not the right Man on our side,
> the Man of God's own choosing:
> Dost ask who that may be? Christ Jesus, it is He;
> Lord Sabaoth His name, from age to age the same,
> And He must win the battle.

When we walk in grace, we can trust that Jesus is directing our thoughts and allowing us to act boldly with carefree abandon. God does at times speak to His children in sensational and mystical ways, but at other times He speaks to us through our thoughts. Don't fail to recognize the miraculous in the mundane. It is exciting when God speaks clearly in ways that leave little room for doubt, but usually He speaks and reveals His will without the help of electrifying phenomena.

The apostle Paul often received visions and even heard God speak audibly at least once. Yet he never sought those kinds of experiences. He trusted the Holy Spirit within him to fulfill God's will. He trusted his own thoughts, declaring on one occasion, "We have the mind of Christ" (1 Corinthians 2:16). Paul didn't agonize over knowing the will of God—he just *did* it! He trusted that his thoughts were actually the thoughts of Christ within him. That sounds like carefree living, don't you agree?

Whose Thoughts Are These?

Often I am asked, "How do I know if my thoughts are coming from God, Satan, or myself?" That's an important question for someone who wants to know God's will. If we are going to take the advice we hear in our minds, we should know where our thoughts originate.

Thoughts from the Enemy

These thoughts are easy to identify. Anything that contradicts the righteous character of God or contradicts the Scriptures comes from our adversary. You "have the mind of Christ," so it's obvious that unholy thoughts don't originate from yourself. Holy people don't produce unholy thoughts. Yet we sometimes *hear* unholy thoughts. Why? Not every thought you have is your own. When an unholy thought comes into your mind, you can be assured it didn't originate there. It was introduced from outside.

It is helpful to know that the enemy introduces thoughts into our minds at times. I remember times in my own life when, while I was praying, a horrible thought would suddenly come into my mind. Have you had that experience? I'd be praying, and unexpectedly a horrible word or idea would pop into my head, seemingly out of nowhere. Then I would say, "Oh God! Forgive me! How could I think about that—especially while I'm praying?" It was such a dirty trick. Satan would introduce a thought to me and then condemn me for having it! Later I found freedom when I realized that while I'm responsible for how I handle my thought life, it is not a sin to *hear* an ungodly thought in my mind.

I was once counseling a man who battled with this problem.

Periodically, blasphemous thoughts would cross his mind. This led him to believe he had committed the unpardonable sin. Yet the man was deeply committed to Jesus Christ. I attempted to explain to him that not all his thoughts were his own, but he didn't understand.

There was another person in the room with us observing our meeting. I leaned toward the man with the problem and motioned for him to lean toward me. I then whispered in his ear, "Do you see Jim sitting there beside you?" He nodded.

"Slap him in the face as hard as you can," I said. The man looked at Jim and then looked at me, bewildered. I waited. He sat there for a moment, looking back and forth. Again I motioned for him to lean toward me, and then whispered, "With an open hand, slap Jim in the face so hard that you knock him off the chair!" (Jim didn't know his vulnerable position at this moment!) Then I sat back. The man looked confused, unsure of what to do.

Finally, I asked him aloud, "Are you going to do it?"

"No!" he answered.

"Well, are you at least going to confess to God that you had such a terrible thought?" I asked.

"No," he said.

"Why not?" I persisted.

"Because *you* said it!" he responded.

"That's right," I said. "And somebody else is saying things to you sometimes too, but you've been taking the blame for it."

Again, it's important to recognize that there is no sin in the *awareness* of a thought. You are responsible only for what you *do* with that thought. In 2 Corinthians 10:5, Paul tells exactly how he dealt with such thoughts: "We are destroying speculations and every lofty thing raised up against the knowledge of God, and we are taking every thought captive to the obedience of Christ." Our defense against evil thoughts is Jesus!

Thoughts from God or Ourselves

What if the thought that comes to mind doesn't contradict the nature of God's holiness? Is it my thought, or God's? The answer is "yes"—it is *our* thought. When we trust in Christ, we can know that our thoughts are the thoughts of Jesus. Remember, we have the mind of Christ. That does not suggest that we *are* Jesus Christ or that we lose our distinct individuality because we are in Him. What it does mean is that Jesus will express His thoughts and actions through our own individual personality.

Those who are abiding in Christ can trust their thoughts and act decisively in life. The fact that you may have doubts doesn't mean that you aren't acting in faith. If there is no room for doubt in your decision, then there is no *need* for faith. To experience God's will, simply trust Christ, and then act in boldness. The rest is up to God.

Does this suggest that our ability to make choices is infallible? Not at all. Yet the potential for making a mistake should never paralyze us from making decisions. As we depend on the indwelling Holy Spirit to guide us, He will intervene at any point where we might unintentionally go astray. He can be trusted to stop us from making the wrong choice.

On at least one occasion Paul found himself at a place where he might have made a wrong choice if the Holy Spirit had not shown him that his intentions were out of line. During Paul and Barnabas's second missionary journey, after they visited Mysia, they decided to move on to their next destination. Luke wrote, "After they came to Mysia, they were trying to go into Bithynia, and *the Spirit of Jesus did not permit them*" (Acts 16:7). How wonderful to know that Jesus within us will *keep* us in the perfect will of the Father!

Knowing that Jesus is expressing His thoughts and actions through you as you trust Him will unload fears from you and empower you to live in a carefree way. If you are depending totally upon Christ to lead you, He will do it! If you start to make a mistake, He won't permit it. A lack of understanding in this area will cause us to move through life in a tentative, almost paranoid manner. But knowing that the Spirit of Jesus will keep us in His will enables us to move forward with enthusiasm, joy, and anticipation. The God who saved you will also guide you! Don't worry about going astray. Simply choose to depend entirely upon Him to guide your steps, and then move out in faith.

I Really Thought This Was God's Will

If Satan can't paralyze us with fear about moving forward in life, he will try to make us think we have missed God's plan. For example, a pastor friend of mine, David, came to me one day and said, "Steve, I really believed that God was leading me to serve as senior pastor at this church when I came. But the way things have turned out, I think I might have missed His will on this one."

David's concerns had arisen because after just a few short months, things weren't moving along in the church as he had expected. In addition, some of the key leaders in the church were already criticizing him. This scared him. "A guy usually gets a short honeymoon in the church before this kind of stuff starts," he said.

David's fear that he had missed God's plan for him is a common concern. We've all often made decisions with certain expectations about the results of our choice. When the results don't turn out the way we hoped, it's easy to think we have somehow gotten out of the will of God. This is a lie that will cause you to become unproductive in spite of the fact that you are exactly where God wants you. When you believe you are out of God's will, you will lose all motivation to act in confidence and faith. Carefree living isn't an option in that mindset.

Maybe you have made choices only to later wonder what went wrong. You prayed about the choices. You evaluated them and then made your decision. Then things turned sour. Does this mean you missed God's will? No. Psalm 37:23 says, "The LORD makes firm the steps of the one who delights in him" (NIV). God *did* direct your steps. Does it make sense that you could have sincerely *prayed* and earnestly *trusted* God to guide you, only to have Him idly sit by and watch you make a mistake? Our loving Father will *not* permit that to happen!

When events don't unfold in the way you want or expect, it simply means one thing: God has a different plan. You aren't out of His will—you are discovering that His will is producing results you didn't expect. A person may argue, "But this *can't* be from God! It's all wrong!" Don't try telling that to Daniel, who found himself in a lion's den after he acted in faith. Or to Paul, who found himself shipwrecked on the island of Malta and being bitten by a poisonous snake while there—*after* he had determined to make his way to Rome to proclaim the gospel in the heart of the empire. John faithfully preached the gospel because he knew that was God's will for him. Consequently he found himself exiled to the isle of Patmos. These examples affirm that when it may *appear* that we are out of God's will, we are actually in the center of His perfect plan for us. *Never* second-guess God's will after you have acted in faith.

The disciples and others might have concluded that God's will wasn't behind the crucifixion of Jesus. Yet beyond the natural reality of a crucifixion on Friday was the coming supernatural reality of a resurrection on Sunday! Although it may have seemed that a mistake had happened, Jesus was *in* God's will as He hung on the cross. Don't conclude otherwise about your life when you find yourself on a cross. *God is in control!* Honor Him by affirming that He has indeed directed your steps even when they led to a place you did not expect.

Pick a Spot and Run!

Imagine yourself standing in the center of a large field with an unobstructed view of the horizon in every direction. To the west you can see the ocean. To the east you can see a beautiful mountain range. To the north is a lush forest. Looking south, you see a beautiful lake shaded by overhanging trees. As you look, you see many small points on the horizon. Those points represent your choices in life. You can go to any one of them; many look interesting, others don't. Which points should you choose? If you are trusting Christ within you, the answer is easy. You can choose any place you desire. Of course, it's important that you are enjoying an intimate union with Jesus at the time you make your choice. In other words, don't act independently of Him. Trust Him to guide your thoughts, and then make your decision!

Have you selected the point on the horizon to which you want to go? Then run! Run there as fast as you can. Run with excitement and joyful anticipation. When you reach the spot you have selected, do you know what you will find? Jesus will be standing there. You'll see His arms outstretched toward you, and He will be laughing with joy. "Come on!" He will say. "Run! Run! I've been waiting for you to get here! This is *exactly* where I wanted you to be!" "Lord!" you exclaim. "I'm so glad you're here! No matter what this place holds for me, I *know* the Father's purpose will be done because You drew me here and will be with me at every moment."

Practice the secret of carefree living and you'll experience the joy that comes from knowing and doing God's will. You don't have to be afraid. Trust Jesus and go forward in faith. As you abide in Him, He will keep you in His will at every moment. He *is* God's will, and you are in Him. You can't go wrong with that kind of arrangement!

 WALKING TOGETHER

Dear Father,

I haven't enjoyed full freedom in Christ because I've been filled with so many of the cares of life. Now I understand that You just want me to walk with You, knowing that the specifics of Your plan will become clear. Teach me to trust You so I make choices in faith, and not fear. Enable me to move forward with confidence. I renounce the fears that have paralyzed me, and I affirm that I trust You to guide my thoughts and desires. I ask You to keep me in Your will, and I praise You that You will do it. By Your grace, I will experience carefree living more and more each day.

GROUP QUESTIONS

1. Discuss the difference between a grace-oriented approach to decision-making and a legalistic approach. Paraphrase Philippians 2:13 in your own words. What would this verse say if it had been written by a legalist?

2. Read Acts 13:1-3. When it comes to knowing God's will, how does the church at Antioch compare with the modern church? In what ways does the modern church seek to *find* the will of God? Describe a specific time when God *revealed* His will to you.

3. In what ways can we cooperate with the Holy Spirit so we can readily know the Father's will? Discuss what it means to be a "living and holy sacrifice" (Romans 12:1-2).

4. How does holding on to personal rights keep a person from experiencing a carefree lifestyle? Discuss a time

when you experienced fear because one of your rights was threatened. How was the matter resolved?

5. What would you tell somebody who says he or she is afraid that Satan's deception may cause him or her to get out of God's will? What verses would you show this person from the Bible?

6. How do believers know whether their thoughts are their own, from God, or from Satan?

7. Describe a time in your life when the Holy Spirit intervened and kept you from making a wrong choice. Also, think of a time when you thought you had made a wrong choice, but later discovered that God had led you all along.

Chapter 8

THE SECRET OF REDEFINING GOD

Emily had come to seek counseling because of personal problems in her family. "I tried God and all that religious stuff," she said. "It just didn't work for me, so I walked away from God."

"Describe God to me," I said. As Emily talked about God, I immediately understood why she had decided to walk away. The god of her imagination was nothing like the One revealed in Jesus Christ. Her god was one whose personality more closely resembled a cruel prison warden than a loving Father.

After further discussion, I discovered that Emily had been reared in a religious home where attendance in a legalistic church was the extent of the spiritual input she received. Between her legalistic church and spiritually dead home, she had developed a concept of God that would repulse anybody.

Emily struggled with a real dilemma. On one hand, she wanted no part of God as she understood Him to be. On the other, she couldn't satisfy the spiritual hunger that gnawed within her. While her mind rejected all things spiritual, her heart cried out for the fulfillment that can only be known through experiencing the life our Father offers.

Emily's hunger for God is a universal condition. Blaise Pascal, the French philosopher and physicist, pointed to an idea that is often paraphrased like this: "Within the heart of every man is a God-shaped void that cannot be filled by created things, but only by the Creator."* People will go to amazing lengths to fill that God-shaped void. If necessary, they will *create* a god in their attempt to satisfy their spiritual longings. This is affirmed by contemporary society's preoccupation with spirit beings, evolved spiritual entities, and a countless number of options from a myriad of world religions.

Perhaps the greatest need in the arena of spiritual development is the need to have a clear understanding of the nature of God. The secret of redefining God doesn't mean we recast Him into an image of our own making. That is precisely the problem that already exists in the world today—even the religious world—even the *Christian* religious world. We have imagined God to be like us, and He isn't. Don't worry about those who warn us of compromising when it comes to how we see God. Too late—it has already happened. The god of our day is a totalitarian despot, not the Loving Father Jesus revealed to us.

What we need is to redefine God, abandoning the way we have wrongly understood Him. Instead, we need an accurate understanding of who He is. How tragic that so many people today have a concept of Him that is far removed from the truth! Many who grew up under the suffocating influence of a rules-based religion can't even begin to comprehend Him as a Father

---

* "...There was once in man a true happiness of which there now remain to him only the mark and empty trace, which he in vain tries to fill from all his surroundings, seeking from things absent the help he does not obtain in things present...But these are all inadequate, because the infinite abyss can only be filled by an infinite and immutable object, that is to say, only by God Himself." From Blaise Pascal, *Pensées*, Section X ("Sovereign Good"), 148.

who is loving, gentle, smiling, happy, and accepting. The god of their minds is harsh, punitive, and distant. They see him as the moral policeman of the universe—watching for infractions that might be committed at any moment. Their god is more interested in matters of right and wrong than anything else, including people.

We have taken Adam's shame from the Garden of Eden and blended it together with the demands of the polluted Christian religion that poses as authentic Christianity. And with those two poisons we have tried in futility to create the pure Water of Life. Then we wonder why our spiritual thirst isn't satisfied and why nobody else wants what we have.

When our focus is on religious performance, it is impossible to see God clearly. It's easier to find the proverbial needle in a haystack than to see God in the middle of the contemporary church world, whose focus is entirely on religious performance.

The God I Invented

Thanks to the influence of godly parents, I was a young boy when I became a Christian. By the time I reached 16 years old, nobody could have been more sincere about his faith than I was about mine. By the time I finished high school, I was as bold as a believer can be. I preached in parking lots at bowling alleys and movie theaters. I witnessed to anything that breathed. About the time I started college, I was introduced to the writings of men like E.M. Bounds, R.A. Torrey, Charles Finney, and others whose testimonies stirred my heart. I had a genuine desire to make my mark for God in this world.

When I was 19 years old, I became a senior pastor. Over the next few years, through nobody's fault but my own, my focus shifted. Gradually I found myself becoming more and more consumed with ministry and less and less with Jesus. I still loved the Lord, but I wasn't *in* love with Him the way I once had been. The work of ministry gradually became my life. I believed that

God had called me to do something great for Him, and I certainly didn't want to let Him down. In small, indiscernible increments I moved away from the Christ-centered lifestyle I had enjoyed and took on a service-oriented lifestyle.

Although I was as sincere as I had always been, a metamorphosis began to occur in my mind. In my perception, the God of my childhood who loved and accepted me unconditionally became a God whose attitude toward me on any given day was determined by how well I served Him. I imagined a God who was more like a divine Employer than a devoted Father. I believed that His blessings came as a result of my faithfulness.

When circumstances were hard, I assumed I was doing something wrong. I would examine my life, looking for deficiencies—which are always apparent when one is absorbed in critical self-examination. Consequently, I felt unacceptable before God because I had so far to go in overcoming my personal deficiencies. The god I invented could never be totally pleased, because I would never be totally perfect. He seldom smiled; in fact, He often appeared frustrated with me.

Recognizing God's Faithfulness

During that time, the fatal flaw in my misunderstanding of God was caused by my emphasis on myself. I believed that my faithfulness caused God to bless me. But now that I understand the grace walk, I know that God's blessings aren't the result of my faithfulness, but because of His. God doesn't bless us because of how wonderful we are, but because of how wonderful He is!

The essence of legalism is the effort to gain God's blessings by what we do. This concept comes right out of an Old Testament mindset and shows no understanding of the covenant of grace. When Moses came down from Mount Sinai with the Law, he gave this message from God to the people of Israel: "Now then, if you will indeed obey My voice and keep My covenant, then you shall be My own possession among all the peoples" (Exodus

19:5). The prescription was clear—do the right thing, and you will be blessed. This method motivated the Jews to try hard to please God by their behavior. Yet in spite of all their efforts, they were always failing to be consistent in their devotion to Him.

By this point in this book, I trust you've learned that God didn't give the Law because He believed that the people would keep it. He gave them the Law to prove that man cannot earn God's blessings—that he is incapable of consistently living a godly lifestyle on his own. God blesses nobody on the basis of merit. Every blessing finds its source in His grace. You can't separate His true identity from grace. In grace He blesses us because we are in Jesus Christ, and for no other reason at all. Sadly, many are miserable because they still live with an Old Testament perspective that causes them to try to stay in God's favor by good behavior.

Law demands, "Your behavior must improve to receive God's blessings!" Grace opens our ears to hear the voice of God saying, "I will bless you until your behavior does improve!" When we redefine who God is in our minds by rejecting the legalistic despot and instead see a Loving Daddy, *then* we become equipped to live a consistently godly lifestyle. Understanding His great love causes our heart to be changed so we are motivated to godly living by desire, not duty. Remember what God said in Ezekiel 36:26-27:

> Moreover, I will give you a new heart and put a new spirit within you; and I will remove the heart of stone from your flesh and give you a heart of flesh. I will put My Spirit within you and cause you to walk in My statutes, and you will be careful to observe My ordinances.

Three times in these verses God says, "I will." That's the meaning of grace. It's not about what we do, but about what He does as a result of His love for us. He promised that He would give us a new heart (desires) and a new spirit (identity). He said that when His Spirit came into union with us, He would cause us to live a godly lifestyle. The grace walk doesn't depend on our feeble efforts, but on His faithful empowerment within us! The real God is a faithful God who will accomplish what He has determined to do in us.

Receiving God's Forgiveness

Perhaps the one obstruction that most prevents people from seeing God's smiling face and resting in His unconditional acceptance is a wrong view of His forgiveness. Our God is a forgiving God, as He proved at the cross. Jesus prayed, "Father, forgive them" while His foes were still driving the nails into His body. He didn't wait for them to ask Him for forgiveness. He didn't even wait for them to change their minds about what they were doing (repent), but forgave them anyway. That kind of forgiveness comes from a source called Grace.

Did you know that your sins have been forgiven? Forgiveness is the deliberate choice to release a person from any obligation he owes as a result of any offense he has committed. God's decision to forgive you originated before you were even born. The Lamb slain from the foundation of the world had bound you up in His heart before you breathed your first breath.

Divine forgiveness doesn't depend on your contrition or your promise to do better. You weren't even in the picture yet when our Triune God set His heart on you. Neither were you there when Jesus took your sin into Himself and paid sin's penalty on your behalf. To be accurate, you weren't there physically, but the reality is that you were "in Him" in the sense that the God who stands outside of time took you, your sins, your spiritual corruption in Adam, your independent ways—He took it all into Himself and suffered the sting of death brought by sin.

You did nothing to deserve to be forgiven. It wasn't because He saw in advance that one day you would be sorry. It wasn't that He forgave you in the hope you would accept it. He simply chose to forgive you. The choice was motivated by His character, not yours. That's the kind of God He is.

God doesn't make deals by offering to forgive us if we "let Him." Grace isn't a two-way contract where both parties have to do their part. It's a covenant made between the Father, Son, and Holy Spirit, who have agreed to unilaterally forgive our sin. We are simply the named beneficiaries of a covenant established long, long ago.

An improper concept of who God is might cause somebody to argue, "Wait a minute! If that's true, you must be saying everybody goes to heaven!" No, I'm not suggesting that. People don't go to heaven because they're forgiven. They go to heaven because they trust in Christ and His finished work. If you've thought God's forgiveness is your ticket to heaven, you've been mistaken.

Paul wrote, "God was reconciling the world to himself in Christ, *not counting people's sins against them*. And he has committed to us the message of reconciliation" (2 Corinthians 5:19 NIV). It doesn't get plainer than that. When God was reconciling the world to Himself in Christ, did He succeed, or was His attempt thwarted in some way? Of course He succeeded. Today, He does *not* count people's sins against them. Isn't that what this verse says?

To declare the forgiveness of sin is to declare the biblical gospel of salvation. Is it necessary for people to believe it? Of course it is, but their failure to believe it doesn't mean God failed in what He did at the cross. Romans 3:3 asks, "What then? If some did not believe, their unbelief will not nullify the faithfulness of God, will it?"

Paul wrote that God has "committed to us the message of reconciliation." What we proclaim is, "You have been forgiven by God! Now, *believe and receive it*!" Without receiving His forgiveness, a person cannot experience the benefits of what He has done, but again, that doesn't mean God failed when He did it. It means they will miss out on the Eternal Party even though we've all been included in it. Even if they are at a dance, deaf people don't usually dance because, even in the presence of the music, they don't hear it.

Sin is now off the table in terms of causing a breach between you and God. Hebrews 9:26 says, "He has been manifested to put away sin by the sacrifice of Himself." That's what the incarnation of Jesus was about, and that's what He accomplished.

We owe God nothing for our sin. He chose to carry the weight of our offense against Him to the cross, and to release us from its demands. It wasn't God who demanded death for sin. It was *sin* that demanded death. "The wages *of sin* is death," the apostle Paul wrote in Romans 3:23. It wasn't God the Father who killed Jesus. It was sin.

When Adam sinned, God came looking for him. Adam must have figured he was in trouble and was going to be punished, so he hid. However, God hadn't told him, "In the day you eat from the tree of the knowledge of good and evil, I will kill you." No! He told Adam, "In the day you eat from it *you will surely die*" (Genesis 2:17)—but it was *sin* that caused Adam to die, not God. Our God doesn't bring about tragic endings by killing. His goal is always to give life because He is life and can do no other. Death will never have the final word over Him.

The secret of redefining God in your mind may set you free to enjoy Him like nothing else ever has. He has poured out onto you the total forgiveness secured by Jesus at the cross. He doesn't ration it out a little at a time. Just as Jesus died for the sins of your whole lifetime, God the Father has granted you forgiveness for all the sins of your lifetime. At this very moment, you stand before God in complete forgiveness. You may be surprised by your sins and expect God to become angry, but your sins don't surprise Him. They have been dealt with in totality. It really *is* finished. You are forgiven.

Asking for Forgiveness

When we ask God for forgiveness of our sins, we imply that Jesus' work on the cross isn't finished even though Jesus clearly said it is. Nonetheless, some people say that the New Testament teaches we are to ask God for forgiveness when we sin. This is where it becomes important for us to "rightly divide the word."

Maria came to talk with me about this issue. "So you're saying I don't need to ask God to forgive me for the sins I commit?" she asked.

"Maria, how many of your sins did Jesus take to the cross with Him?"

"All of them."

"That's right. Because of His perfect sacrifice our sins have been dealt with completely."

"But some verses talk about confessing our sins," she replied.

"Yes, but to *confess* is different from asking for forgiveness. To confess simply means to agree. I'm not suggesting that we don't admit it when we've sinned. What I'm saying is that we now live under the New Covenant, and all our sins have been forgiven once and for all. Jesus took them all into Himself so we would be free."

"Okay…but what about when He taught the disciples to pray, 'Forgive us our trespasses as we forgive those who trespass against us?'"

"Who was He speaking to right then?" I asked.

"Well, to His disciples," she responded.

"Yes, and which covenant did they live under at that time?"

"The New Covenant, I suppose. After all, Jesus came to bring in the New Covenant," she answered.

Maria didn't understand when the New Covenant actually came into force. She thought that it started at the beginning of the New Testament Scriptures. That's a common misunderstanding. However, the covenant did not actually start until the death of Jesus.

Why? Because the Covenant of Grace was the last will and testament of Jesus Christ. The age of grace could not become operative until He died. The writer of Hebrews declares,

> Where a covenant is, there must of necessity be the death of the one who made it. For a covenant is valid only when men are dead, for it is never in force while the one who made it lives (Hebrews 9:16-17).

Both Scripture and common knowledge tell us that a will does not come into force until the one who made it dies. Given that fact, which covenant was in operation during the whole lifetime of Jesus? The Covenant of Law. Jesus lived under the Old Testament Covenant. The new began at His death, not at the beginning of the Gospel of Matthew in the Bible.

Remember that the purpose of the Law was to raise the awareness of sin among the Israelites. Because Jesus lived under the Covenant of Law and was sent to those under the Law (see Galatians 4:5), His words often reflected that covenant. Such is the case when He discussed the matter of forgiveness. In Matthew 6:12, when Jesus responded to His disciples' inquiry about how to pray, He said this about forgiveness: "Forgive us our debts, as we also have forgiven our debtors." He elaborated on forgiveness under the Law system in verses 14-15 by saying, "If you forgive others for their transgressions, your heavenly Father will also forgive you. But if you do not forgive others, then your Father will not forgive your transgressions."

This was the Law in action—if you want God to do something for you, then you must first do something to cause Him to act in your behalf. Under Law, if there was even one person you hadn't forgiven, then you couldn't be fully forgiven yourself.

When asked about forgiveness, Jesus answered according to the Law. Yet in His personal relationships, he always acted in grace. An example of His approach is illustrated in John 8, where we read about the woman who was caught in the act of adultery. When the scribes and Pharisees pointed out that the Law of Moses commanded that adulterers be stoned, Jesus didn't dispute this. He simply suggested that the scribes' and Pharisees' application of the Law include themselves. After His challenge that the sinless one among them cast the first stone, the crowd dispersed until no one was left except the woman. Having acknowledged the validity of the Law at that moment, Jesus went on to demonstrate gracious forgiveness toward her by asking, "'Woman, where are they? Did no one condemn you?'

"And she said, 'No one, Lord.'

"And Jesus said, 'Neither do I condemn you; go your way. From now on sin no more'" (verses 10-11).

This incident is so typical of the Lord Jesus during His earthly ministry. He utilized the Law to raise the awareness of sin and then demonstrated grace by His own behavior.

Under the Covenant of Law, a person was not totally forgiven. He or she had to receive ongoing forgiveness in order to remain in a guilt-free state. But at the cross, God poured out all His forgiveness on us. We don't need to ask for more! Paul describes total forgiveness in Colossians 2:13-14:

> When you were dead in your transgressions and the uncircumcision of your flesh, He made you alive together with Him, having forgiven us *all our transgressions*, having canceled out the certificate of debt consisting of decrees against us, which was hostile to us; and He has taken it out of the way, having nailed it to the cross.

This verse shows that the sins of your lifetime were nailed to the cross with Jesus, and *all* of them were dealt with then and there. If you believe that your sins are still being forgiven one at a time as you confess them and ask for forgiveness, there's a troubling question you must consider. What happens if you die with just one sin in your life that you haven't thought to ask

Him to forgive? The truth of Scripture is that before we were born, God saw our lives and identified every sin we would commit. Jesus carried all those sins to the cross with Him, and God canceled the debt. Every sin of our lifetime has been forgiven—past, present, and future! There is no sin left with which you can be charged—and no Law to charge you even if there were.

Are you still living as if you were under the Old Testament Law by constantly asking for God's forgiveness? Those days are over and finished! Rejoice in the truth that you are totally forgiven. The Old Covenant is forever gone. The writer of Hebrews said,

> If that first covenant had been faultless, there would have been no occasion sought for a second. For finding fault with them [the people of Israel], He says,
>
> > Behold, days are coming, says the Lord,
> > When I will effect a new covenant
> > With the house of Israel and with the house of Judah;
> > Not like the covenant which I made with their fathers
> > On the day when I took them by the hand
> > To lead them out of the land of Egypt;
> > For they did not continue in My covenant,
> > And I did not care for them, says the Lord.
> > For this is the covenant that I will make with the
> >   house of Israel
> > After those days, says the Lord:
> > I will put My laws into their minds,
> > And I will write them upon their hearts.
> > And I will be their God,
> > And they shall be My people.
> > And they shall not teach everyone his fellow citizen,
> > And everyone his brother, saying, "Know the Lord,"
> > For all will know Me,
> > From the least to the greatest of them.
> > For I will be merciful to their iniquities,
> > And I will remember their sins no more (Hebrews 8:7-12).

The day described in this passage is the day in which we live! The secret of redefining God is seeing Him as the One who has forgiven us for every sin of our lifetime! The cross of Jesus was God's final word about our sins. As far as your sins go, it really *is* finished.

Resting in God's Favor

Until we realize we have been totally forgiven, we will never experience the freedom to enjoy our relationship to God and our fellow man. Our faulty belief about forgiveness will make it necessary to constantly focus on ourselves, scrutinizing our every thought and action. In mandating the habit of continual asking for forgiveness, legalism redirects the focus from God to self. Whenever we have a false concept of God that sees Him as a stern Judge, we are preoccupied with our own behavior. But the secret of redefining God the way Jesus revealed Him to us frees us to simply revel in His loving acceptance.

I spent 29 years of my Christian life in self-examination. I often asked for forgiveness for things I had done that I shouldn't have done, as well as for things I didn't do that I should have done. Sometimes I even asked God to forgive me for sins I had committed that I didn't even know about. I wanted to cover all the bases. There's a word for that kind of lifestyle: *bondage.* When I came to realize God's total forgiveness of me, for the first time I was free to see Him as He is—a smiling, loving Father. Until then I stared at myself and imagined Him looking down at me with a frown.

Knowing God's Personality

Personality types have been categorized in as many ways as we can imagine. A myriad of sources offer an abundance of personality tests that are supposed to help discern a person's temperament.

Have you ever wondered what God's personality is like?

How would you describe it? Some people might suggest that we can't know His personality, but that wouldn't be true. God has revealed Himself to us through His Son, Jesus. They're just alike because they are one.

Stop reading and consider this question for a moment: *What if God is nothing like I have imagined Him to be?* Did you think about that for a moment? I asked you to pause because we only hurt ourselves when we hold on to any wrong perceptions about God. The sooner we redefine who He is and have a right view, the more easily we'll see His smiling face. Are you willing to have your mind changed concerning what He is like? Consider the following descriptions of His personality.

He Is a Loving and Laughing God

God delights in you. The heart of the Lord is ecstatic about us. Zephaniah 3:17 gives us a glimpse of His exhilaration over us: "The LORD your God is in your midst, a victorious warrior. He will exult over you with joy, He will be quiet in His love, He will rejoice over you with shouts of joy." What an exciting thought! The God of the universe is so thrilled with you that He is overwhelmed with joy. Unable to contain His emotion, He shouts for joy when He looks at you.

You may not feel like God has such great admiration for you, but He does. In Ephesians 2:10, you are called God's workmanship. By placing you into Jesus Christ, God has made a beautiful new creation out of you. You deeply stir His divine passions. Nothing will ever change that fact.

You can relax and enjoy Him. There is nothing you can do that would cause God to love you any more or any less than He does right now. He has decided to love you, and nothing will change that.

I first met my wife when I was 16 years old. I have already described how excited I was about my first date with her. On the day of that date, I went to great effort to cause her to like me. As soon as I came home from school that Friday, I drove Dad's car around into the backyard. I filled a pail with dishwashing detergent and went to work cleaning that car. I scrubbed it from top to bottom. I used tire black on the tires to make them shiny. I sprayed a special finish on the interior. I vacuumed the carpet. That car was clean.

About two hours before I was to pick her up, I began to get groomed and dressed. I showered and put on my navy-blue pants and my light-blue shirt—I even wore a tie. I wanted Melanie to like me! I soaked myself in cologne and drove to her house. I arrived early, so I circled the block until it was time to pick her up. When I pulled into her driveway, I checked my hair, sprayed breath freshener in my mouth, and sprinkled some more cologne on myself and on the side of the seat where she would be sitting. (I hoped it would get to her.) I walked up to the door and rang the doorbell. When her mother came to the door she invited me in, telling me that Melanie wasn't quite ready. "Oh, that's okay," I gushed. "I don't mind waiting at all!"

After a while Melanie walked into the room. I stood up and told her how beautiful she looked. As we walked to the car, I rushed ahead to open the door for her. I wanted her to like me. After the movie we went to eat. "Order anything on the menu," I said. "Do you want to get the large pizza with all the toppings? We can do that." I really wanted this girl to like me. She did.

Three years later I married her. The months passed. With time, my words and actions changed. I was saying, "You'd better get in the car! I'm not going to be late for church again. I'll leave you. I mean it!" Then at the restaurant: "You know, we could just go to the drive-through at McDonald's. They'll sell those Happy Meals to adults!" I even let her open the car door for herself. I reasoned that I had her love now, so there was no need for all that "dating stuff" anymore.

Needless to say, by the end of our first year of marriage, conflict was common. Over a period of months as I prayed about our relationship, God revealed some things to me. I came to understand that I wasn't to serve my wife so she would love me, but because it was a way to express my love for her. Soon I began to act differently toward her, and our marriage changed. I've been opening the car door for her now for over 40 years—not so she will love me, but because I love her. I'm not obligated to serve her through considerate gestures now. I'm free to do those things because I can rest secure in her love for me.

Do you know that you can relax and enjoy God's love without trying to earn it? When we know how much He loves us, it frees us to serve Him out of gratitude and love for Him. God loves you whether or not you open the car door! Service is difficult if we are trying to earn His favor, but it becomes a pleasure when it is a natural expression of the intimate relationship we share with Him.

He Is an Accepting and Affirming God

Not only does God love you, but He also likes you. You don't need to improve for Him to accept you. He saved you while you were still in the filth of your sins. Do you think that now He doesn't like you because you haven't reached perfection? "As high as the heavens are above the earth, so great is His loving-kindness toward those who fear Him" (Psalm 103:11).

Human beings often accept other people on the basis of qualities that they like. Sometimes we believe that God relates to us in the same way we tend to relate to others. "You thought that I was just like you," God said in Psalm 50:21. But He isn't like us.

How do you see God in your mind? Do you see the possibility that you may need to allow the Holy Spirit to redefine who He is for you? Maybe you grew up in a home or church where you came to believe things about God that simply aren't true. Maybe you have gotten stuck in Old Testament texts that have shaped an understanding in your mind about who He is.

Do we throw those Old Testament passages out? No, of

course not. What we *do* choose to do, however, is to formulate our understanding of God the Father by what Jesus showed us about Him. Hebrews 1 says,

> In the past God spoke to our ancestors through the prophets at many times and in various ways, but in these last days he has spoken to us by his Son, whom he appointed heir of all things, and through whom also he made the universe. The Son is the radiance of God's glory and the exact representation of his being, sustaining all things by his powerful word (verses 1-3, NIV).

Based on these verses, consider these two questions:

1. How is God revealing Himself to us "in these last days"?

2. How does Jesus' revelation of His Father compare to the way sunbeams reveal the sun?

Is the Old Testament a part of the inspired Scriptures? Of course it is! However, there are many aspects of the Old Testament that sincere Bible students wrestle with in an attempt to understand God. On the other hand, Jesus has *clearly* revealed His Father to us. My point here isn't to dampen your interest in the Old Testament Scriptures but to whet your appetite to understand your Father through the lens of the Son, Jesus! The Old Testament certainly isn't wrong, but neither is it complete. Jesus *is* the complete revelation of the Father. It would be absurd to think He left out a whole other side of God that He didn't bother to reveal. No, you don't have to worry about that. "If you have seen [Him], you have seen the Father" (see John 14:9).

Watch how Jesus acted during His earthly ministry. God isn't angry. He isn't judgmental or punitive toward us. His heart has always been inclined toward us.

When you finish this chapter, put the book down for a moment and close your eyes. Embrace the secret of redefining God. Imagine Him looking at you. He is smiling, at times laughing out loud with joy. It is evident that the reason for His happiness is you! You can see the pride in His eyes. He adores you, and it is obvious. One glimpse of His smiling face and you know that for time and eternity, you are acceptable! Now, hold on to that reality for the rest of your life.

WALKING TOGETHER

Dear Father,

Open my eyes so I can see You clearly. Tear down every false imagination I may have about what You are like, and redefine Yourself to me. Cause me to understand how You really feel about me. I confess I have judged You wrongly by failing to recognize and appreciate how much You love and accept me. Thank You for forgiving all my sins. Empower me to live in confidence and boldness, knowing that You are working on my behalf in every circumstance of life.

GROUP QUESTIONS

1. Emily decided to walk away from God because "it just didn't work" for her. Her concept of God was partially formed by the input she received at a legalistic church. Describe what a legalistic church is like. What are the differences between a church built on legalism and one built on grace?

2. What would you say to somebody who continues to struggle with guilt over past sins? What Bible verses

would you show to this person? How does God feel about us when we sin?

3. Explain the difference between an Old Covenant and New Covenant understanding of forgiveness. When did the New Covenant begin? Why did Jesus tell His disciples they would not be forgiven unless they forgave everybody who had offended them? Is that true for today? Why or why not?

4. Read Colossians 2:13-14 and paraphrase the passage in your own words. How is it possible that God could forgive sins you haven't even committed yet? If future sins are already forgiven, what keeps us from living a lifestyle of continuous sins?

5. Describe God the way you have imagined Him to be. Have you redefined Him in your own mind after reading this chapter? If so, how?

6. Read Zephaniah 3:17 in several different translations of the Bible. List three characteristics of God's character given in this verse.

7. Write a prayer to God acknowledging how He feels about you (not how you feel about Him).

Chapter 9

THE SECRET OF KNOWING YOU'RE INCLUDED

Imagine being a young adult so deep in debt that there is no way to become financially free in your lifetime. Envision, for as long as you live, always having bills larger than your paycheck. There is no way out. All you can do is hope to survive another month.

Then one day you receive an official-looking letter from a prestigious law firm. You open the letter and discover that a distant relative has died. The attorney is notifying you that in accordance with the terms of the will left by the deceased, all of your financial obligations have been paid in full. You no longer owe anything to anybody. Even your mortgage has been paid off. Can you imagine how excited you would be? You would probably talk about it constantly for weeks to anybody who would listen.

After a while, although you would still be grateful, you wouldn't talk about the incident all the time anymore. And over the next 30 years, you manage to do moderately well financially. You no longer experience poverty nor debt, but at the same time, neither have you enjoyed the luxuries of life. Your finances have provided an average lifestyle—nothing more and nothing less.

One day you receive a telephone call from someone who introduces herself as an investment advisor at a bank. "I wanted to discuss your account with you," she says. "I don't have an account at your bank," you say politely. She states your full name and asks, "Is that the person to whom I am speaking?" "Yes," you answer, "but I don't have an account there." She asks you to verify the address in her records. It doesn't seem familiar at first, but then you realize it's the address of your distant relative who died 30 years earlier. "That is the address to which we've been sending your statements all these years," she responds. As the conversation continues, you discover that the executor of your rich relative's estate had opened an account in your name 30 years ago.

"How much is in the account?" you ask, curious.

"Brace yourself," says the banker. "The account has grown to several million dollars! Apparently the attorney who notified you about your debts being paid off failed to mention that you had also been left a very generous inheritance."

How would you feel upon receiving such news? For 30 years you have lived a very modest lifestyle while, all along, you had the resources in the bank to live in the lap of luxury! You'd probably be wondering, *Why didn't that attorney tell me the whole story? Why did he fail to tell me about the wealth I inherited?*

The Whole Story

I was always thankful that the debt of sin was paid by Jesus Christ when He was my substitute on the cross. I knew I would never feel the sting of death that sin brings, thanks to Him. Yet it was not until I had been a believer for many years that I heard the complete story of salvation. I understood that the debt sin demanded had been paid, but I didn't know the rich inheritance that was mine through the death of Jesus on the cross.

There is more to the New Testament gospel than many of us realize. Somehow over the past 20 centuries, the church has dropped the ball. We have talked much about the topic of forgiveness by God. Sadly, we've almost ignored the best part of the gospel. We have often led people to believe that being forgiven is the pinnacle of their faith. That we've been forgiven is an awesome reality—but it isn't God's ultimate purpose in salvation.

Jesus didn't come to earth and die just so we could be forgiven and go to heaven. That's the common belief among religious people, but the truth is much better than that. Salvation isn't about heaven. *It is about Him.*

Make no mistake about it—forgiveness is wonderful, but the greatest aspect of what Jesus has done overshadows forgiveness. What could possibly be greater than to know that our sin has been taken away from us? It is to know that in Christ we have become children of God. The New Testament message of our identity is that we are "in Him."

Our adoption in Him was the eternal purpose our Triune God had in mind all along. The coming of Jesus into this world wasn't a reaction to what Adam did in the Garden of Eden when he sinned. The story of redemption doesn't begin with Adam. It predates Adam all the way back to a time when there was no date! It was our God's plan to bring us into His family before the first second existed in this human dimension we call "time." When there was no "space" there was already Grace. You were in His heart before the first molecule was spoken into being.

Before Adam sinned, the Lamb slain from the foundation of the world had assured your safe delivery into His arms. As numerous theologians have said, "You were found before you were lost." Your adoption in Jesus Christ is the result of a love set on you long before the first ray of light exploded out of the mouth of Christ and started its race across the universe. The gospel is the good news that you are included in the victory Jesus accomplished over sin and death.

You were included even before you knew or believed you were included. Even when you stood in the darkness of unbelief there was a "true Light which, coming into the world, enlightens every man" (John 1:9) and you stood blindly in that Light of Love. People without sight can't see the light, but it shines on them nonetheless. You may have lived all eternity with a darkened mind and never have known the Light, but He knows you. The light of His love has always shone on you.

Your faith in Christ isn't the tipping point that causes the efficacy of His finished work to be real. Your faith is a response to a Reality that existed when you didn't even know what you didn't know. "I have loved you with an everlasting love; therefore I have drawn you with lovingkindness," God says to you (see Jeremiah 31:3). Speaking of His crucifixion, Jesus promised, "When I am lifted up from the earth, I will draw everyone to myself" (John 12:32 NLT). "Everyone" includes you.

In Jesus Christ you have been adopted—given the *full standing* of a son—by the Father Himself. It is "by *His* doing you are in Christ Jesus," Paul told the Corinthians (see 1 Corinthians 1:30). It's not because of anything you do. *Nothing* you do has caused you to be placed into Christ Jesus. That happened as a result of a divine act of grace.

With bated breath, all of heaven watched until the fullness of time came and, in the person of Jesus, the eternal plan our Tri-une God had held in His heart forever came bursting into time and space like brilliant rays of sunshine penetrating the blackest clouds.

"When the fullness of the time came, God sent forth His Son, born of a woman, born under the Law, so that He might redeem those who were under the Law, that we might receive the adoption as sons," Paul proclaims in Galatians 4:5. How could such a thing happen to us? "He predestined us to adoption as sons through Jesus Christ to Himself, according to the kind intention of His will," Paul explains in Ephesians 1:5.

Does that include you? According to the Scriptures, "Christ also died for sins *once for all*" declares the apostle Peter, "the just for the unjust, so that He might bring us to God, having been put to death in the flesh, but made alive in the spirit" (1 Peter 3:18).

Paul, the great apostle of grace, tell us that "the death that He died, He died to sin *once for all*" (Romans 6:10). The New Testament makes the bold claim that the death of Jesus Christ happened one time and included everybody (see also Hebrews 7:27; 9:12; 10:10).

Am I suggesting here that everybody will go to heaven? Does all mankind's inclusion in the work of Jesus mean that people have personally experienced salvation and will enter heaven without faith in Christ? No, it does not. That is a Universalist position and not the view I am presenting here.

Jesus Christ's Finished Work

What our inclusion does mean is that there's nothing left to be done, neither for us nor by us, because Jesus has done it all! The gospel doesn't become true because we believe it. To the contrary, we believe it because it is true. The gospel isn't a sales pitch but an announcement of good news. It's not *potentially* good news. It is *present-moment good news for all of humanity*. The news is, "You have been adopted in Jesus Christ by His Father! Now, believe it! Receive it! Thank Him for it and live like it's true because it is!"

Nobody who refuses to receive Jesus Christ can personally experience the benefits of the cross, but that doesn't mean Jesus failed in what He did there. In some ways, people who refuse Christ are like the elder brother in "the story of the prodigal son" in Luke 15. While a party is going on inside the house, this boy was standing in the darkness refusing to enjoy what was freely offered.

When Jesus Christ said, "It is finished," He was telling the truth. It *is* finished. To experience the benefit of His finished work, we need only believe it. Some would argue that belief itself is a work, but that is nonsense. Belief is nothing more than the joyful response to something that is true, in a way that allows us to participate in the reality embodied in that truth. Consider an example:

On January 1, 1863, President Abraham Lincoln signed the Emancipation Proclamation, which set free every person held in slavery in the Confederate States. When he signed that paper, it was a done deal. It was "finished." Were all the slaves free? Yes, they were. The authority and work of the president made it so.

The sad reality is, however, that many slaves didn't benefit from that proclamation. Many didn't know of it. Others didn't believe it. Consequently, despite the fact that there was nothing left for Lincoln to do because he had done everything for them already, those slaves did not *experience* the benefit of Lincoln's finished work in setting them free.

So it is with those today who don't accept the finished work of Christ. It *is* finished, but until they believe it, they won't experience the benefits of what He has done. Although their adoption is real, their acceptance of that reality is necessary, or they will never enjoy the blessings that are already theirs through Christ.

Hebrews 4:2 explains the situation well: "Indeed we have had good news preached to us, just as they also; but *the word they heard did not profit them, because it was not united by faith in those who heard.*" It's true whether people believe it or not—but it will not profit them apart from faith.

A Man with the Whole Message

The apostle Paul was consumed with a great desire to see people understand this gospel. He explains his calling in Colossians 1:25-28:

Of this church I was made a minister according to the stewardship from God bestowed on me for your benefit, so that I might fully carry out the preaching of the word of God, that is, the mystery which has been hidden from the past ages and generations, but has now been manifested to His saints, to whom God willed to make known what is the riches of the glory of this mystery among the Gentiles, which is Christ in you, the hope of glory. We proclaim Him, admonishing every man and teaching every man with all wisdom, that we may present every man complete in Christ.

Paul said that he wanted to fully preach the message God had given him. He wanted to proclaim the full message of God—to leave nothing unspoken that needed to be said. His goal was to present his converts mature in Christ.

The word "mystery" could actually be rendered "secret." It refers to something that wasn't known before, but has now been unveiled and made plain. What was this great secret of grace Paul was revealing to those who hadn't known it? It was that God had made known just how rich in grace He is by including the Gentiles (non-Jews) in His redemptive purpose—to the dismay of many in Israel. Many Jews didn't like it, but Paul described it as "the glory of this mystery [secret]." "It's not just Jews," Paul said. "We're all included." To experience the benefits of what Jesus did, these Gentiles simply had to believe just like we do today, and the efficacy of the cross was as complete for them as it was for the Jews.

The secret of inclusion is a glorious truth to many people, but like the Jewish religionists of Paul's day, some do not like it. If you accept the good news that everybody is included in Christ's finished work, you risk the contempt of those who don't believe it. You can make your best efforts to help them see you aren't suggesting that we're all Christians, or that we believe everybody has experienced salvation and is going to heaven whether they believe or even want it—but some still won't accept this good news. Worse yet, they will accuse you of distorting the gospel. No amount of words will clarify the matter for minds that are resolutely closed to it. Only the Holy Spirit can open hearts. Our role is simply to boldly proclaim. The results are up to God.

Living As One Included

The gospel of salvation is factual, but your salvation experience has not become *actual* to you until you come to understand that the mysterious oneness you share with Christ leads to a radical adjustment in how you live. If you have been fully evangelized, you will know you are *energized* with divine life for today. Grace tells the whole story by offering dynamic power for living by the life of Jesus.

Although you may know that your debt to sin has been paid, you will never fully experience the supernatural empowerment of God's life until you understand that Christ is not simply *in* your life—Christ *is* your life! Your body is nothing less than a container for divine life. As you trust Him, that life flows out of you continually.

We are designed both to contain and release divine life so we can make a mark on this world with the love of God. We need the revelation that Paul prayed would be granted to the Ephesians:

> I pray that the eyes of your heart may be enlightened, so that you may know what is the hope of His calling, what are the riches of the glory of His inheritance in the saints, and what is the surpassing greatness of His power toward us who believe (Ephesians 1:18-19).

We understand the gospel when we know the riches we have inherited by receiving the life of Jesus Christ. Some people have said, "When you have Jesus Christ, you have everything you need." That is exactly right, but what practical good does it do to have everything you need if you don't even know what you have? Many people don't understand how rich they are in Him.

Your Official Notification

In case you haven't already received the news, I want to notify you of something from which you may greatly benefit. This news offers you the chance to experience a brand-new life, filled with privileges that are "far more abundantly beyond all that [you could possibly] ask or think" (Ephesians 3:20). If you act on the following information, your life will never be the same. There is nothing you must do to gain the benefits. The only condition is that you believe the message and receive the inheritance that has been left for you.

You already know about the death of Jesus Christ on the cross. You understand that on the cross He took the penalty sin brings into Himself, and it has been paid in full. By the shedding of His blood, your sins are forever gone.

That isn't the whole story, though. Jesus left a last will and testament outlining the riches He wants you to enjoy as your inheritance. In this New Testament, the bequest is explained. This news may sound too good to be true, but you can believe it because these promises were made by God the Son, witnessed by God the Father, and will be implemented in your life by God the Holy Spirit. Consider these benefits you have inherited in Christ Jesus:

You Have a New Life

Have you ever wished you could be somebody else? Well, you are! Jesus has stepped into the dead, Adamic life that was yours before He came and has conquered it. In its place He has given you His life.

You have been made into a brand-new person (2 Corinthians

5:17), who has been created as one who is totally righteous (Ephesians 4:24). You are now holy (1 Corinthians 3:17), not because you did anything to deserve it, but because righteousness has been given to you as a gift (Romans 5:17). You still have the same body, but a new you lives inside! Christ is your life now (Colossians 3:4).

Don't be deceived into believing this isn't true just because your behavior hasn't indicated it to be so. Your actions don't define you. Your God has defined you by placing you into His Son. *Jesus defines you.* When you know who you are, you will find the power to behave in a way that is consistent with your true identity. It is a matter of renewing your mind to the truth through faith in Christ so that your lifestyle will be transformed (Romans 12:2).

You Have Power over Sin

Before Jesus died and left us this spiritual fortune, none of us had power to overcome sin. We were doomed to be its slaves forever. Now things have changed. You have a new nature—His! Because His life is within you, He will enable you to overcome sin as you depend on Him. Remember that you died with Christ (see Romans 6:1-6). You were placed on the cross in Jesus Christ and crucified there with Him. Not only did He die, but you died too—your life now consists of Christ in you (see Galatians 2:20). "He who has died is freed from sin" (Romans 6:7).

To experience power over sin, simply relax and trust in the sufficiency of Jesus Christ at every moment and recognize that you are dead to sin. Whether you feel it or not, "consider [yourself] to be dead to sin, but alive to God in Christ Jesus" (Romans 6:11). Act like it's true because it is! When you depend on Jesus and act in faith, you will see for yourself that you are dead to sin.

Imagine a guy named Leo overdosing on cocaine and dying. They take his body to a funeral home and prepare it for burial. A few hours before the funeral starts, one of his drug buddies comes into the parlor where they have Leo's corpse laid out. Nobody else is in the room, so his buddy walks up to the casket and leans over. "Hey, Leo," he says, "we're alone right now, man. I've got some good stuff here in my pocket." He reaches into his pocket and pulls out a small bag of cocaine. "Look, man, it's pure. Take a snort," he says, putting the bag under his buddy's nose. "What's your problem, man? Here, I'll put a little on my finger for you to taste. You'll see—it's good stuff."

Do you know what Leo's response is to all this? Nothing. He's just lying there. If he could speak at that moment, do you know what he would say? "Hey, stupid! I'm dead! Can't you see that?" Dead men don't want cocaine, even if they loved it before.

The Bible clearly teaches that one part of our inheritance is that we have died to sin. You can sin if you choose, but when you awaken to the reality of your God-given identity you will discover that you don't want to live a life of sin anymore. You died to all that. Now you are alive to God. *He* motivates your desires and interests. You finally have power over sin!

You Have a New Freedom

If you haven't known your identity in Christ, you haven't experienced freedom. When you don't know your authentic identity, you will wrap your life up in rules, thinking that rules will produce a greater quality of spiritual living. But in reality, as Romans 7:10 tells us, religious rules always prove "to result in death." "A sinner saved by grace"—what a pitiful description of a person who possesses the very life of Jesus Christ! God prefers to call you a *saint*. That's how He refers to you 63 times in the New Testament. Why would we want to identify ourselves by the word *sinner* when Jesus came to deliver us from our sin?

As you experience the secret of your inclusion in Christ, you will discover a freedom like you've never known. Paul said, "All things are lawful for me, but not all things are profitable" (1 Corinthians 6:12). This kind of statement almost scares a legalist to death. "I am free to do whatever I want?" That's right. Trust Christ to live His life through you, and do whatever you want to do.

What would happen if the spirit of Babe Ruth suddenly came into you? Do you suppose that you might find yourself overwhelmed with the desire to become a professional ballet dancer? Babe Ruth in tights—it's a scary thought. If wagers were placed on what you would do if the essence of Babe possessed you, the odds wouldn't be high on the chance that you would take up ballet. It just doesn't fit. I think we all know what you would want to do.

As you grow in confidence about your inclusion in Christ, you don't have to worry about religious rules. Legalistic religion makes people afraid that if they don't build their lives around rules then they will suddenly find themselves consumed with a desire to live a lifestyle of sin. They need to understand the implications of their inclusion in the life of Jesus Christ. Their new nature has become one with the Holy Spirit so that when they are by faith walking in the Spirit, God's desires become their desires. A person possessed by the Holy Spirit no more wants to live a lifestyle of continuous sin than someone possessed by Babe Ruth wants to take up a lifestyle of ballet. God's plan is for you to trust the Holy Spirit of Christ to animate your behavior. You don't need to try to gain something from your Father. You are "in Him" and that gives you full access to everything you need now and forever.

 ## WALKING TOGETHER

Dear Father,

I believe the secret of inclusion. Open the eyes of my heart so I may see the full implications of the reality that I am included with Christ in Your love, acceptance,

*and goodness! Don't stop until I fully know who I am
in You! I want to experience everything from You that
can be known in this lifetime.*

❧ GROUP QUESTIONS

1. Discuss the differences between a partial
understanding of the gospel and the complete gospel.
List a few truths that you believe are typically missing
from a complete presentation of the gospel.

2. What distinguishes what you read in this chapter
from Universalism—the view that everybody is
automatically saved and is going to heaven when they
die?

3. Why did Jesus come into this world? What are the
negative results present in the life of a person whose
understanding of salvation goes no further than
receiving forgiveness and going to heaven?

4. Read Colossians 1:25-28 and discuss what it means to
fully carry out the preaching of the Word of God. What
is the mystery that "has been hidden from the past ages
and generations"?

5. What happened at the cross in terms of our identity?

6. Read Romans 6:1-7. What does it mean to be dead to
sin? If we are dead to sin, why do we still sin? What is
God's method for enabling us to experience victory
over sin?

Chapter 10

THE SECRET OF LOOSENING UP

After I resigned my role as the pastor of a local church in 1994, our family found itself in a situation we had never faced. Because I had been in pastoral ministry since the age of 19, we had always attended the church where God had led me to serve. Now it was necessary for us to select a church. We wanted to find one that our family could call home.

During our search, we visited one church that reeked of spiritual death. The problem wasn't their form of worship. I've seen God reveal Himself in many churches that practice many different forms of worship. The problem at this particular place was the absence of life. A person could easily conclude by the tone of the service that they had just received late-breaking news: *It was all a big mistake. Jesus didn't rise from the dead after all. Sorry, folks.* Have you ever been in a spiritually dead environment? If so, you know exactly what I am describing.

After the service ended, our family went to a local pizza restaurant. When we walked in the front door, a friendly greeter welcomed us. As we sat down at a table, the cheerful atmosphere in the place immediately struck me. People were smiling and laughing together. Some were singing along with the mechanical characters that were on the stage to entertain the children. Our server was outgoing and seemed anxious to make our visit an enjoyable one. I found my mood being elevated just by being there.

Later as I thought about our experiences that morning, I concluded one thing: I had no interest at all in becoming a part of the church we had attended, but if the restaurant had extended an invitation for me to join, I might have moved my membership there! The staff there seemed to enjoy life. They seemed to care about our needs. No doubt about it—they could have made a Pizzabyterian out of me that day!

Where Is the Enjoyment?

The seventeenth-century English reformers said, "Man's chief end is to glorify God and enjoy Him forever." Look around at Christendom today and you'll see that most of us either didn't get the notice about our "chief end" or for some reason just can't seem to experience that enjoyment. That's why the secret of loosening up, which we'll discuss in this chapter, is so important.

Enjoying life is the prime directive given to us by Jesus Christ Himself. "I came that they may have life, and have it abundantly" (John 10:10). An abundant life is a fulfilling, overflowing life. It's a life filled with meaning and fulfilled purpose. Religion crushes us under the weight of demanding expectations, but Jesus said He came to give us an abundant life.

The problem we have today is that we have become trapped in a legalistic perspective. It focuses entirely on doing the right things and avoiding the wrong things. That outlook has put many people into a paranoid, self-absorbed, fearful frame of mind that leaves no room for enjoying life. It robs us of the ability to relax and just *be*, and it coerces us into being obsessed at every moment with what we *do* in an attempt to meet the job description we wrongly imagine God has mandated for us.

It also produces a judgmental attitude toward anybody else we think might not be toeing the line, based on what we think they should be doing. A person who isn't able to relax and enjoy life doesn't understand, or often appreciate, others doing it either.

God's kingdom is a perpetual celebration of Life. We were created to enjoy the eternal interpenetration of life and love shared among the Father, Son, and Holy Spirit. That is your reason for existence—to share in His life. When by faith we consciously participate in that circle of love, we are experiencing life as it is intended to be.

Think about it—at this very moment you are firmly situated in the embrace of the Triune God. Nothing can touch you without going through Him. You have been irrevocably joined together in this divine union. The One who loves you eternally holds you, accepts you and, in fact, is delighted with you. Because of your adoption in Jesus, the Father looks at you and says, "This is My beloved child, in whom I am well pleased!"

Can you imagine what would happen in our lives if we all accepted this reality and lived as if it were true? The experience of living in that place is the antidote to fear and worry, insecurity and doubt, and judgmentalism and criticism. To recognize our home in that Triune Circle is to finally sigh the great sigh of relief—the relief that can only be known when we truly understand that we and every detail of our lives are held firmly in the arms of the One who loves us more than anything. For those who have been trapped in the suffocating world of dead religion, the outcome of grasping that reality is that they are finally able to stop following the rules and start living.

The Party Poopers

Until we live out of the reality of grace, we will forever be judgmental toward everybody, including ourselves. Do you remember the attitude of the older brother in the story of the prodigal son? The prodigal had gone to the far country and wasted his inheritance on wild living. Not once does Jesus suggest that he made a wise choice, but the wisdom of the son's choice wasn't the point of the story. The Father's grace is the focus of that parable. When the younger son came to his senses and returned home, his dad received him back with enthusiasm and joy. He even threw a party in his honor. Luke describes the reaction of the older brother, who valued living by the rules above everything else, including his younger brother:

> Now [the] older son was in the field, and when he came and approached the house, he heard music and dancing. And he summoned one of the servants and began inquiring what these things could be. And he said to him, "Your brother has come, and your father has killed the fattened calf because he has received him back safe and sound." But he became angry, and was not willing to go in (Luke 15:25-28).

That older brother needed to loosen up! All he could see was the wrong that had been done. He was blind to the fact that his younger brother was home, safe and sound. He was *home*! But the older brother's obsessive-compulsive connection to the rules caused him to miss the joy of a fellow-brother come home. He didn't like the situation—not at all.

There is no bigger party pooper than legalism. Because it focuses us so much on performance, those who are trapped in it can't understand the kind of grace that would cause a father to receive a son whose actions fell short of the standard he has set for himself and others. The legalist relates to people with a condescending attitude, judging them on the basis of his own lifestyle. His performance may look good, but inwardly he is wasting away because his focus on rules and performance has robbed him of authentic joy in life. He has no time for music and dancing; there's work to be done! The devil never takes a break—why should he? A legalist is never a genuinely happy person. When he sees others dance to the music, he can't stand it.

The prodigal son's older brother is a perfect model of how this attitude looks in religious snobs today.

1. The older brother separated himself because his younger brother didn't live up to the standards he embraced. He refused to be involved in the same party with one who had failed so miserably. Jesus ran *toward* sinners, but people like this brother run *from* them. Separation—exclusion—that's their style.

2. The older brother's relationship to his father revolved around doing the right things and not breaking his commandments. He said, "For so many years I have been serving you, and I never neglected a command of yours" (Luke 15:29). He knew no sense of closeness to his father because his whole focus was on behavior. That's what it's all about to the person bound up in legalistic religion. It's about serving and about obeying commands. Rules are what matter, not relationships.

3. Finally, the older brother resented the grace his father showed to the prodigal. He pointed to his own faithfulness and said, "When this son of yours came, who has devoured your wealth with harlots, you killed the fattened calf for him." There are people today who still find it hard to even call anybody a brother who doesn't live up to their own standards. The elder son called his brother "this son of yours." Today, that same religious arrogance causes some to believe it's wrong to unconditionally accept somebody who has sinned. After all, they reason, when we do, we are condoning his or her behavior!

Fun Faith

Many people who go to church every week have the same elder-brother attitude. I'm reminded of someone who thought a local church shouldn't give a baby shower to a young lady there who had become pregnant before she was married. Forget compassion—there are *convictions* that have to be maintained here! Sadly, this viewpoint is prevalent in the world of religion, including the "Christian religion" (which is actually an oxymoron).

In the story Jesus told, the heart of the prodigal's father seems to parallel that of our heavenly Father. He loves to celebrate when someone comes back to Him in repentance. His focus isn't on balancing the books for the wrong done. With a gracious Father, there is no record keeping of right and wrong. Love "keeps no record of wrongs"! (See 1 Corinthians 13:5 NIV.)

Please note that when I refer to the prodigal's repentance, I'm not referring to his coming home. That wasn't when he repented. In fact, that wasn't repentance of any kind. He simply came home with a new game plan. His motivation was that he was hungry, so he determined to ask his father to forgive him while promising to do better. His approach was like that of the person today who, in the same way, begs God's forgiveness and promises to do better.

The father wouldn't even listen to that drivel. Our Father isn't interested in it either. The whole time the boy was trying to give his rededication talk, his dad was hugging him; laughing, shedding tears of joy, and shouting to his servants, "Make all the preparations! We're going to have a party!"

The younger son's repentance didn't come until he stopped his silly attempt to gain favor from his father by expressions of remorse and promises of recommitment. He abandoned that effort and at last melted into his father's embrace, realizing there was no need for him to do anything. All this talk about remorse and recommitment was unnecessary. His uptight attitude about doing better was as bad as his older brother's. Both of them needed to loosen up and realize it was the love manifested in their father that put them in a good standing, not their good or bad behavior. Does behavior matter? Of course it does. Ask the prodigal. Does it change how a gracious father feels toward his son? No, it does not.

Grace doesn't condone sinful behavior, but neither does it punish somebody who has sinned. They have already been punished *by sin itself.* The last thing they need is more condemnation. Instead, what they need is unconditional acceptance and love.

Contrary to what some tightly wound religious people believe today, faith and fun are not in opposition to one another. Even under the Old Covenant, God made provision for His people to celebrate:

> You shall eat in the presence of the LORD your God, at the place where He chooses to establish His name, the tithe of all your grain, your new wine, your oil, and the first-born of your herd and your flock, in order that you may learn to fear the LORD your God always…If the distance is so great for you that you are not able to bring the tithe…then you shall exchange it for money…You may spend the money for whatever your heart desires: for oxen, or sheep, or wine, or strong drink, or whatever your heart desires; and there you shall eat in the presence of the LORD your God and rejoice, you and your household (Deuteronomy 14:23-24,25,26).

Contrary to the opinion of some people, God loves fun! In eternity past, the three Persons of the Trinity all enjoyed intimacy with each other. It was a private party among the Father, Son, and Holy Spirit. Back then, before the beginning of time,

God determined to host a universal party. He would create man for the purpose of sharing His life with him, thus bringing him into that Eternal Party. Today, our privilege is to invite people to get up and dance with Grace!

The father of the prodigal said, "We *had* to celebrate and rejoice, for this brother of yours was dead and has begun to live" (Luke 15:32). When a dead person comes to life, what can you do but celebrate? The Bible teaches in Ephesians 2:1 that there was a time when "you were dead in your trespasses and sins," but now Jesus Christ has made you alive. This is a reason to party!

Some people today seem to have forgotten that the activity of the early church revolved around parties. The Greek word for it is *koinonia*, often translated as *fellowship*, but that word sounds too churchy to some contemporary ears. There's nothing inappropriate about using the word *party* as a modern paraphrase of the word.

Many parties celebrate life: a birthday party celebrates the years a person has lived; anniversary parties celebrate a couple's life together; a graduation party celebrates the start of a new life for the graduate. Parties are focused on and full of life. Doesn't that description describe New Testament Christianity as well? Its essence is a celebration of divine life. In Adam we were dead, but in Christ Jesus we have been made alive! It's appropriate to "shout joyfully to the LORD" and to "serve the LORD with gladness" (Psalm 100:1-2). In other words, it's time to loosen up and have a party!

Parties Attract People

The growth of the early church in Acts is inseparably linked to the fact that these early Christians continuously integrated celebration as a part of their daily lifestyle. They were consumed with an explosive joy that could not be squelched. Their lifestyle was an ongoing celebration of Jesus and their life in Him. "Day by day continuing with one mind in the temple, and breaking bread from house to house, they were taking their meals together with gladness and sincerity of heart" (Acts 2:46).

These people had an uninhibited, exhilarating enthusiasm about life. They weren't so tightly wound as some people think those who follow Christ should be. In fact, on the day of Pentecost, when the Holy Spirit came upon them, they exhibited such excitement that the crowd thought they were drunk. Onlookers stood in absolute "amazement and great perplexity, saying to one another, 'What does this mean?' But others were mocking and saying, 'They are full of sweet wine'" (Acts 2:12-13).

These believers weren't drunk on wine; they were totally intoxicated with the life of Christ being expressed through them by the Holy Spirit. They were experiencing exactly what Paul meant when he said, "Do not get drunk with wine, for that is dissipation, but be filled with the Spirit" (Ephesians 5:18). These Christians partied "under the influence" of God's Holy Spirit all the time! They celebrated the life of Jesus in everything they did.

The secret of loosening up requires that we stop taking life too seriously. I don't mean we are to be irresponsible or live a careless lifestyle of sin. What we do need, though, is to stop living like we're on trial all the time. You can *rest* and know that you are in a right standing with God and nothing can ever change that. That knowledge won't cause you to sin. To the contrary, it will motivate you to laugh, live, and love in carefree abandon.

Just lighten up and live your life! If it's an action Jesus can empower you to do, then do it with enthusiasm and joy! People are tired of stale religion and tired of those who lug it around with them all the time. But when they see a person who has a consuming passion for life that comes from Jesus, they sit up and take notice. If you want to represent Christ well, then loosen up and have fun! People just can't resist a party. The early church helped introduce many people to Christ because the believers were so in love with Life that others couldn't help but see the difference. They understood that Christ wasn't just a part of their life. In every aspect of daily living, He *was* their Life!

Living Under the Influence

It is interesting that the apostle Paul linked the effects of being drunk and the influence of the Holy Spirit in the same verse. Drunkenness is a prominent part of many parties in our society. Yet in Ephesians 5:18, Paul asserted that people are not to be possessed by the power of alcohol, but rather are to surrender the control of their faculties to the influence of the Holy Spirit. What we have to experience in Him is a greater high than the strongest alcohol could offer.

To fully experience the life we have been given in Christ is to be "drunk on life." Consider these characteristics of a person who is "under the influence":

- *A person under the influence loses all inhibitions.* Have you ever seen somebody try to calm a drunk who is excited? It's almost impossible to do it. He can't be silenced. That's how it is when a person is filled with the Holy Spirit and a love for Jesus Christ. That person *loves* life and expresses it in a panoramic way.

  To live life loud and large in the Spirit is the essence of New Testament evangelism. This isn't a particular personality type but an excitement about Jesus that is contagious. It doesn't take an extroverted temperament for this to happen either. When we are overwhelmed by His grace and caught up in life in Him, people are bound to take note and be drawn to Christ in us, regardless of our personality type.

  Have you ever noticed how that when somebody else laughs you find yourself starting to laugh with him or her? That's how it is when the joy we have in Christ spills out into our daily lifestyle. People will want to have what you have. Religious rules about evangelism will become irrelevant. You won't have to "witness" (verb) to others. You will *be* a "witness" (noun). (See Acts 1:8.)

- *A person under the influence becomes very expressive.* People under the influence of alcohol typically become more animated in their behavior. An angry drunk may begin to behave in a belligerent way. A happy person who is intoxicated may begin to act very happy. Alcohol seems to magnify the underlying trait that a person is exhibiting.

When a person lives from grace, the Holy Spirit magnifies the One who is within her. Grace will cause her to behave in a way that reveals the godliness of her inner character. The life of Jesus Christ within her will come out without inhibition or restraint. Again, this isn't a matter of personality type. Don't think you have to have an outgoing personality. Jesus will express Himself through each of us in the way that is unique to us, but He will be seen.

Loosen Up!

Our God is a party God! Those who feel that the idea of Christians "partying" seems somehow irreverent might benefit from a study of what the Bible says about joy in the kingdom of God. The Lord said, "My servants will shout joyfully" (Isaiah 65:14)! One of the last things Jesus told His disciples concerned having a festive heart: "These things I have spoken to you so that My joy may be in you, and that your joy may be made full" (John 15:11). In His final prayer before going to the cross, Jesus prayed "that they may have My joy made full in themselves" (John 17:13).

May we once again rise up in celebration! We have been forgiven of our sins (Ephesians 1:7). Jesus Christ is our very Life (Colossians 3:4). Nothing can separate us from the love of God

(Romans 8:35-39). We will always triumph in life (2 Corinthians 2:14). It's time to loosen up and party!

There is a tragic lack of joy in the lives of many today because they are willing to settle for happiness. Happiness depends on happenings. People are happy when the circumstances of life are to their liking. While pursuing happiness is the primary goal for many, it isn't a high priority to God for us to be happy. He wants to give us joy. Happiness depends on external circumstances; joy runs much deeper than that. Happiness comes from the outside into us, but joy comes from the inside out. It is a pleasure that flows from our innermost being—an inner sense of well-being and contentment produced by an awareness of our life in Him. Joy is unaffected by our surroundings.

Joy exists in a different dimension than happiness. Consider Paul's time in the jail at Philippi. He wasn't happy to be there. Later, in the letter he wrote to the church he founded in that city, he said that he had "the desire to depart and be with Christ, for that is very much better" (Philippians 1:23). Jail—where he again sat when writing his letter—was no thrill for him. Yet the theme of his letter to the Philippians was that of rejoicing. Repeatedly he echoes the message "rejoice in the Lord" (Philippians 3:1). In prison, Paul might not have felt the happiness that circumstances provide, but he definitely experienced the joy that came from his connection to Jesus Christ. He understood that "to live is Christ and to die is gain" (Philippians 1:21). His life wasn't joined to the external, but the Eternal. He wonderfully demonstrated that a person could experience joy without happiness.

You are in Christ, so join the party! Loosen up and live! God won't mind. In fact, He has been waiting for you to enjoy the celebration. Go ahead and let go. Believe it, live it, sing it. Celebrate! Celebrate! Get up and dance to the music of His grace!

🦋 WALKING TOGETHER

Dear Father,

*I have allowed myself to become too rigid, too uptight.
I want to experience the joy of my union with You. Free
me from everything that keeps me from joining the
party. I've been bound up far too long. I want to loosen
up and experience life to the fullest. By faith, I receive
the fullness of joy that Jesus prayed that His followers
would possess. May that joy overflow from my life.*

🦋 GROUP QUESTIONS

1. "Man's chief end is to glorify God and enjoy Him
   forever." Discuss what it means to enjoy God. Is it
   possible to glorify Him without enjoying Him? Identify
   some practical ways we can glorify and enjoy Him.

2. Read the story of the elder brother in Luke 15:25-32.
   List the three characteristics of legalism reflected in
   this son's life that are mentioned in this chapter. What
   other characteristics of legalism are demonstrated by
   his attitude and actions? Can you identify with any of
   these characteristics?

3. Identify the elements of a party that are presented in
   Psalm 100. What other passages in the Bible illustrate
   the celebration that exists in the kingdom of God?

4. Identify verses in Acts that show people being drawn to
   Christ because of the celebration that existed among
   the Christians there.

5. Read Ephesians 5:18 and Acts 2:12-13. What
   similarities do we see between being under the
   influence of alcohol and under the control of the Holy
   Spirit?

6. How can it be proven from the Bible that God is "a party God"? Find a few verses suggesting that a party is happening in heaven continuously.

7. Define *happiness* and *joy*. What are the differences between the two? Can you think of a time in your life when you experienced joy but were not happy?

8. Why do some people associate the secret of loosening up with the tendency to slip into a sinful lifestyle?

Chapter 11

THE SECRET OF ALL SECRETS

This book has presented ten secrets rooted in grace that can transform your life. Individually, they have the capacity to give you a greater sense of peace and internal rest than you may have ever known until now. Collectively, they could turn your world upside down by facilitating such a radical change in you that you won't recognize yourself once that change has taken place. I know this from personal experience.

I have changed so very much over the past 25 years. I look at myself now and find it hard to believe that my beliefs and practices back then seemed so right and so important to me. I am a man set free. I still have a long way to go in my own grace journey, but I am not where I used to be. Some people who have known me all these years may think that's a shame. Others rejoice with me. The wonderful thing is that I'm not controlled anymore by what people think. I have been acted upon by a Power who was too great to resist. At least to me, resistance seemed futile and ultimately seemed foolish. I have consciously been swallowed up in a Group Hug that makes everything else look pale by comparison.

Do you want to embrace the secret of grace outlined in this book? If you've had significant religious indoctrination in your life, some of these chapters may seem questionable to you. Maybe you have had mental reservations about certain aspects of grace discussed here. You may struggle with the ideas I've shared, but deep down inside you surely must hope they could be true. How wonderful would it be if grace really were like this? The good news is, *it truly is like this!*

The secrets of grace described in the previous ten chapters aren't principles to apply to your life. They aren't paradigms for living that you need to embrace. Neither are they goals to achieve. Each is an individual part that together makes up the whole. The whole is what I refer to in this chapter as "the secret of all secrets."

The Best News You'll Find in This Book

I've saved the best until last in this book. The ten "secrets" discussed in the previous ten chapters find their source in the Secret of All Secrets, who is Jesus Christ. The ten are all part of the One. He personifies all the aspects of grace discussed here. Let us conclude your time with this book by showing how it is Jesus who embodies the secrets of grace.

1. The Secret of Not Trying

When you read the first chapter about "the secret of not trying," did it resonate with you, or did you find yourself resisting the idea that life could be lived without committed determination? Here's what Jesus said about the matter:

> Are you tired? Worn out? Burned out on religion?
> Come to me. Get away with me and you'll recover
> your life. I'll show you how to take a real rest. Walk

with me and work with me—watch how I do it. Learn the unforced rhythms of grace. I won't lay anything heavy or ill-fitting on you. Keep company with me and you'll learn to live freely and lightly (Matthew 11:28-30 MSG).

Does the way Jesus described the lifestyle He gives sound as if it requires that we be bound and determined to live a certain way, no matter how hard it might be? Does it sound like something you must *try hard* to do? "Keep company with Me and you'll learn to live freely and lightly," is the way He described it. Jesus Himself didn't try to live for His Father. He recognized His Father's life within Himself and simply lived His life in a naturally supernatural way. The secret of not trying is Jesus. We simply rest in Him and let Him live through us. The secret is in *trusting Him.*

2. The Secret of Weakness

Jesus didn't rely on His own strength when He lived in this world. He openly acknowledged, "By myself I can do nothing" (John 5:36 NIV). "The words that I say to you I do not speak on My own initiative, but the Father abiding in Me does His works" (John 14:10).

His was a life of dependence upon His Father. On the day of Pentecost, when Peter described the great things Jesus did, he said, "Jesus of Nazareth was *a man* accredited by God to you by miracles, wonders and signs, *which God did among you through him,* as you yourselves know" (Acts 2:22 NIV).

It wasn't great human strength that animated the life of Jesus. "He had no beauty or majesty to attract us to him" (Isaiah 53:2 NIV). It was the life of His Father flowing through Him that empowered Him. This approach is so far removed from the contemporary mindset, which focuses on the need for more strength. Our problem isn't that we need more strength.

The problem is that we have too much confidence in personal strength and need to learn the life of dependence like Jesus lived.

When we pray to be made stronger, our prayers contradict the plan our Father has for us. The Bible says, "God hath chosen the weak things of the world to confound the things which are mighty" (1 Corinthians 1:27 KJV). Paul wrote, "When I am weak, then I am strong" (2 Corinthians 12:10). The secret of weakness is Jesus. He submitted His weak humanity to the Father and lived from His strength. That describes the way we can live too.

3. The Secret of Union

The theological phrase *hypostatic union* refers to Jesus' humanity and deity in one person. He said, "Anyone who has seen me has seen the Father" (John 14:9 NIV). "I and the Father are one" (John 10:30). There was no separation between the Son and His Father. Neither is there a separation between God and you.

The knowledge of the oneness we share with our God is perfectly aligned with the relationship Jesus described when He talked about the vine and the branches in John 15. The apostle Paul wrote, "The person who is joined to the Lord is one spirit with him" (1 Corinthians 6:17 NLT). The Father, Son, and Spirit are one. That's what the Bible teaches. You have been joined together with the Son through your adoption in Him and thus are one with the Father and Spirit too. So the secret of union is, again, Jesus. We live as one with our Triune God.

Does this mean that we have become deity too? It doesn't mean that at all, but it does mean that we have "become partakers of the divine nature" (2 Peter 1:4) and can never live a lifestyle separated from Him again. "What shall separate us from the love of Christ?" Paul asks at the end of Romans 8. Then in the closing verses of that chapter, in eloquent words that thrill the heart, the apostle assures us that nothing "will be able to separate us from the love of God, which is in Christ Jesus our Lord" (verse 39).

The same union is yours that was true of Jesus, who was filled with the Spirit and found His source for living in the Father. See yourself as literally in union with God. Act like it, expressing in faith that it's true, and watch the transformation that will come to you.

4. The Secret of a Religion-Free Lifestyle

Although twenty-first-century Christian institutions may resist it, this one is a part of the Secret of All Secrets too. He, Jesus, wasn't a religious person. In fact, His greatest opponents were religious people. He constantly stayed in trouble with the religious leaders because He refused to jump through the sectarian hoops they used to define what godliness looked like. He caricatured their complaints like this: "We played the flute for you, and you did not dance; we sang a dirge, and you did not mourn" (Matthew 11:17). Jesus danced to a Melody they could not hear, and that galled them.

Be aware that when you live in this sort of Jesus-freedom, you'll experience the same kind of criticism He did. Religious people have expectations for you, and they won't like it at all when you refuse to dance to their sour tunes. That's okay. As you live in Jesus, you'll hear the Rhythms of Grace (remember from a few pages back what Jesus said in *The Message* paraphrase of Matthew 11:28-30?), and you'll dance to a Melody that people made deaf by dead religion can never hear. Your Dance Partner will be proud of you too.

5. The Secret of Doing What We Want

Do you think for a minute that Jesus didn't do what He wanted to do? He *wanted* to glorify His Father. And when we experience Him living His life through us, our desires will be the same. The thing religious legalism can never teach you is that *grace creates new desires.*

If you think your core desires are to do wrong, you don't know yourself. The Father has kept the promise He gave through the prophet Ezekiel:

> I'll give you a new heart, put a new spirit in you. I'll remove the stone heart from your body and replace it with a heart that's God-willed, not self-willed (36:26-28 MSG).

That's exactly what the Lord did, and that's why Paul could write, "Thanks be to God that though you were slaves of sin, you became obedient from the heart to that form of teaching to which you were committed" (Romans 6:17). When you know your heart—your authentic self—you can do what you want because your wants will be generated by His indwelling life.

But what if you don't know your real heart-identity? In that case, you're going to do what you want anyway. As you've learned in this book, religious rules don't squelch sin. They stimulate it (see Romans 7:5). The good news is that after you've failed enough times and are sick and tired of the way you're behaving, you'll be in a position to see that a sinful lifestyle isn't your heart's desire after all. Your loving Father will patiently wait for that moment to come and, when it does, He'll be there to heal and help you.

The secret of doing what we want is Jesus. When He lives through you, there is no need to squelch your desires. They come from Him. "Delight yourself in the LORD; and He will give you the desires of your heart" (Psalm 37:4). He will put your desires within you.

6. The Secret of the Right Focus

Jesus embodies this aspect of the secret of grace too. From the time He was a child, His focus was on His Father. An account from His childhood demonstrates this to be the case. It comes from the second chapter of Luke.

The extended family of Jesus went to Jerusalem for the Feast of the Passover. After staying a few days, they left to go home. Apparently Jesus' parents assumed He was with other members of their extended family. After a day on the road, they realized their son was missing and went back to look for Him. After three days they found Him in the temple conversing with the leaders there. Naturally, his mother scolded Him and asked why He would do such a thing. The answer Jesus gives in Luke 2:49 shows the focus of His life from the time He was a boy. I like the way *Young's Literal Translation* renders the verse: "Why is it that ye were seeking me? Did ye not know that in the things of my Father it behoveth me to be?" It's as if Jesus were saying, "What did you expect? Don't you know by now where My focus is? I *had* to do this."

His entire life reflected that resolved focus. He wouldn't take His eyes off His Father and the purpose He had for Him. As He was nearing the finish line for His redemptive mission here on earth, the Bible describes His focus this way: "As the time approached for him to be taken up to heaven, Jesus *resolutely* set out for Jerusalem" (Luke 9:51 NIV).

Can you see that the secret of the right focus is Jesus? As we focus on Him, the same resolve He had to conquer sin once and for all will manifest itself in our own personal lives. We won't experience victory over temptation because of our own will-power but because our focus is on Him. He gives us the resolve to live in a way that honors Him as we focus on Him. You won't sin while fixing your eyes on Jesus. His resolve will be yours. That's a secret worth knowing!

7. The Secret of Carefree Living

Can you imagine Jesus worrying about anything? Why would He? He, more than anybody, understood that His Father was in control over every detail of His life. That didn't keep Him from experiencing normal human emotions. He cried at times, became angry at times, and laughed at times. However, in the midst of the emotional ups and downs of life, Jesus was never filled with concern.

The Secret of All Secrets wants you to know peace in the midst of your troubling circumstances too. The irony of this statement is that He doesn't give you peace, "for He Himself is our peace," as Paul wrote in Ephesians 2:14. Peace isn't a product, but a Person.

As you look at your life and try to gaze into your future through the fog of limited knowledge, know this: you can live a carefree life, "casting all your anxiety on Him, because He cares for you" (1 Peter 5:7). The peace of God that surpasses understanding is yours in Jesus Christ. You don't have to have all the answers. You don't even have to have clarity because you have Him. He has all the answers and it's all perfectly clear to Him. So relax. Stop worrying. Commit your cares into the hands of the One who completely loves you and is working things out for your good. He is the secret of carefree living. Trust Him.

8. The Secret of Redefining God

When Jesus came into this world, He came to a people who were completely confused about the nature of the Father. They saw Him as a God who had strict standards and little patience for those who didn't meet those standards. The god of their imagination was a god who was more interested in their behaving according to his rules than anything else. Read the Old Testament and you'll see they were afraid even to be near Him. In fact, they were even scared to come close to Moses when he had been close to God (see Exodus 34:30).

Jesus turned their concept of God upside down. He constantly said and did things that didn't fit their understanding. Even something as basic as His calling God *Abba* was a shocker to them. They didn't relate to that kind of familiarity with God. They needed to have their personal definition of God redefined. The Secret of All Secrets has come to reveal the heart of His Father to us. Does your concept of who the Father is align with what was revealed in Jesus? Are you still hung up on an Old Testament, blurry-at-best view of who the Father is? Well, don't stay bogged down in Old Testament texts that may leave you confused about the nature of God.

Hebrews 1:3 says about Jesus, "He is the radiance of His glory and the exact representation of His nature." The word "radiance" could be translated as "out-raying." Jesus is to the Father what a sunbeam is to the sun. He is the *exact* representation of the Father.

How can we reconcile those Old Testament verses that seem to portray a very different picture of God with what Jesus revealed? We can't, but don't let limited human understanding trap you in a bad place. While there is much we can't understand, we *can* understand that Jesus was the exact representation of His Father. There isn't a dark side to the Father that Jesus omitted showing to us. Trust the Secret of All Secrets to define for you who your God is. Don't fall backward with "Yes, but the Old Testament says…" There may be things you don't understand there, but you do understand Jesus. Are you going to let things you don't understand take precedence over what you *do* understand? When you see your Father as He is revealed in Jesus Christ, your life will change for the better.

9. The Secret of Knowing You're Included

Dead religion always leaves people struggling to gain acceptance from God. In the Christian religion, it often starts with something we do—praying a prayer, being confirmed, being baptized, or something else a particular tradition might require. The good news is that your connection to God didn't start with you. It began in Jesus Christ long before you were a remote thought in any human mind.

The Bible says, "Even before he made the world, God loved us and chose us in Christ to be holy and without fault in his eyes" (Ephesians 1:4 NLT). How could we think something *we* did caused that? According to this verse, your inclusion in the Triune Circle of Love was decided before the world was made.

It sometimes thrills people to believe this is true about them, but they refuse to believe it about others. The relevant question you must settle in your mind is, *Who does God love?* I believe He loves everybody. That view leads me to believe Jesus died for everybody. We're all included in the cross. Christians, Jews, Muslims, Buddhists, Hindus, and everybody else—we are all included.

This viewpoint runs the risk of being characterized as Universalism, but I am not a Universalist. I affirm the necessity of trusting in the finished work of Christ in order to experience salvation and go to heaven. However, the exclusionist attitude that often exists in churches today is not biblical. The Secret of All Secrets has included everybody in what He has done. That's just how Grace works!

The Bible says, "*While we were God's enemies,* we were reconciled to him through the death of his Son" (Romans 5:9 NIV). It didn't happen when we believed but when He died on the cross, *while we were God's enemies.* It was accomplished "through the death of his Son," not through something we have done. The whole world is now invited to believe it, but we believe it because it is true, not so it will become true.

When you see that everybody is included in what Christ has done, it will transform the way you view other people and allow you to proclaim Christ's finished work with confidence, inviting people to believe in His grace, experience salvation, and know the Secret of All Secrets. He has included us all.

10. The Secret of Loosening Up

So many people wrongly think that to take their faith seriously means they have to forgo relaxing and simply enjoying life. The Secret of All Secrets showed us better than this. The first miracle He ever performed was when He turned water into wine at a wedding party. It isn't without meaning that this was His first miracle. Maybe one intended lesson here is that He wants us to enjoy life.

Religionists didn't like this about Jesus then any more than they like it today. They falsely accused Jesus of being a drunk and a glutton. They didn't like the friends He chose to associate with. "The Son of Man came eating and drinking, and they say, 'Look at him! A glutton and a drunkard, a friend of tax collectors and sinners!'" is Jesus' acknowledgment of the accusations of His critics (see Matthew 11:19 ESV). Apparently He didn't care, because He didn't change His behavior for them.

Many believers today are afraid to loosen up and enjoy life animated by the Spirit. The main cause of this reluctance isn't biblical reasons. Rather, believers know they'll experience what Jesus did when He broke the religionists' rules. They're afraid of criticism from other people. They know all too well that to step across religious boundaries is risky business if acceptance is your highest priority.

The Secret of All Secrets didn't seem to care about all that. To the contrary, He ignored the legalistic religious mores of His day and just lived. You can do the same thing.

Critics will warn you about slippery slopes, about ruining your testimony, about separation from the world, about a dozen other things, all of which will subtly steal your joy if you let it happen. Don't worry about it. Believe me, for every religious person who rejects you there will be *many* others who are attracted to you—or actually, to the Christ who is in you. You will reach more people with God's love by living in freedom than religious people will ever reach from their own captivity.

I give you, the reader, credit for having enough sense to know I'm not advocating a hedonistic lifestyle. I will offer no caveat with this truth. Such a word of caution would reveal an implicit fear that you might get it wrong without a qualifying warning. I have no such fear because I trust the Holy Spirit of God within you.

"Go, eat your food with gladness, and drink your wine with a joyful heart, for God has already approved what you do" (Ecclesiastes 9:7 NIV). Life isn't a test but a rest, so relax and enjoy it. Grace takes the day, every day in your life.

In his "Seventh Homily on First John," the church father Augustine of Hippo gave this pastoral advice: "Once for all, then, a short precept is given thee: Love, and do what thou wilt." In the years since, many have tried to moderate Augustine's comment, but he was right. The secret of loosening up is to cast off the religious straitjacket you may have worn for a long time and live the abundant life Jesus has given you.

Will some people abuse this kind of advice? Of course they will, but the potential for abuse doesn't dilute the power of the truth. You are free, so loosen up! Stop acting religious in an attempt to show your faith. It isn't necessary. The only thing that evidences authentic faith in God is love. If you doubt that, read 1 Corinthians 13, where the Bible makes clear that love is *the* benchmark of a righteous lifestyle. Love God. The rest is just details that His Spirit will work out in you.

The Secret of Grace Is Yours

Did you notice this book's subtitle on the front cover? "Stop following the rules and start living." That's a scary step to take for those who have been indoctrinated with religious legalism. *What will cause them to behave if they don't live by the rules?* Just to ask the question is to reveal little understanding of the transforming power of the grace of God that dwells inside us.

That's the problem today. Many don't know His grace. They only know the rules-keeping system they've lived in and lived by for a long, long time. They've come to believe that life is all about pleasing God by living a certain way—and in so believing, they have missed the point altogether.

Your Father *is* pleased with you, and it has nothing to do with what you do or don't do. He is pleased with you because you have been adopted as His child in Jesus Christ. You aren't big enough to mess that up!

Maybe you're scared that if you stop living by the rules and embrace grace, your lifestyle will jump track and you'll end up in a ditch. Your fear is understandable if you've been indoctrinated to fear true freedom. That fear, however, is without ground.

Jude wrote his short epistle to warn people about the dangers of false teachers and false teaching. After all he has to say on the subject, he comes to the very end of his letter and says this:

> Now all glory to God, who is able to keep you from falling away and will bring you with great joy into his glorious presence without a single fault (verse 24 NLT).

Note the things Jude says God will do:

1. *He will keep you from falling away.* You don't have to worry about being misled. Your God will protect you when your heart is toward Him.

2. *He will bring you to the place of great joy.* Do you have that now? Nothing kills joy like rules. Why not abandon that rules system right now and instead trust in the *relationship* you have to God?

3. *He will bring you into His glorious presence.* This isn't just talking about when you get to heaven. God will make you aware of His presence *now* if you'll abandon the religious rules regime and trust Him instead.

4. *He will bring you to Himself without a single fault.* You don't have to try to improve yourself through adherence to rules. Your God of grace is working in you, and His intention is to bring you to the awareness of your own innocence before Him.

The Secret of All Secrets has your best interest at heart. Give yourself to Him, "being confident of this, that he who began a good work in you will carry it on to completion until the day of Christ Jesus" (Philippians 1:6 NIV). It's not up to you. It never has been. It's up to Him.

A Word from the Author

If reading *The Secret of Grace* has encouraged you, I would be happy to hear from you. Our purpose at Grace Walk Ministries is to share the liberating message of what it means to be in Christ and have Him live His life through us each day. We share this message through teaching in local settings, through radio, television, the Internet, books, audio-video resources, and mission outreaches.

At the time of this publication, Grace Walk Ministries has offices in the U.S., Canada, Mexico, Pakistan, Australia, Argentina, and El Salvador. Our leadership team members are all great communicators and are passionate about sharing the message of our God's loving grace. If you would be interested in having any of our team or me speak to your church or group, please feel free to contact us at the address below.

I also invite you to visit our website at www.gracewalk.org, where you can learn more about our mission and how we are carrying it out across the world. On the home page of our website, you can also watch "Grace Walk," a Bible teaching I share each week that remains available online throughout that week.

You may contact me as follows:

Dr. Steve McVey
Grace Walk Ministries
PO Box 6537
Douglasville, GA 30135
Phone: 800-472-2311
E-mail: info@gracewalk.org
Web address: www.gracewalk.org

May God continue to bless you in your own grace walk as you come "to know Him and the power of His resurrection and the fellowship of His sufferings" (Philippians 3:10).

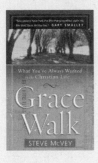

Grace Walk
What You've Always Wanted in the Christian Life

Nothing you have ever done, nothing you could ever do, will match the incomparable joy of letting Jesus live His life through you.

As you relax in Him and delight in His love and friendship, you'll find that He will do more *through you* and *in you* than you could ever do for Him or for yourself. Today is the day to let go of doing and start *being* who you are. Today is the day to start experiencing the grace walk.

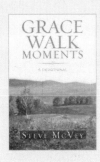

Grace Walk Moments
A Devotional

In these few quiet moments alone, let God remind you of His love and care for you. Experience a taste of what He offers you—refreshment, joy, and complete acceptance.

After all, the grace of God isn't about struggling to be perfect. It's about letting the Father love you and work in you and through you. These devotions will help you understand what He has already accomplished *for* you in Christ and what He longs to do *in* you today.

Helping Others Overcome Addictions
How God's Grace Brings Lasting Freedom
Mike Quarles, coauthor

Immerse yourself in the basic, addiction-breaking truths of God's Word! If you want to effectively help someone, or if you yourself are struggling, the authors show you how freedom from addiction is found only when people fully believe what God says about who they are.

In this book you'll see that freedom from addiction is found not in a program, but in a Person—Jesus, God's Son, the One who can truly set people free.

Includes helpful material on codependency, as well as advice for setting up recovery/support groups for those gaining freedom from addictive behavior.

The Grace Walk Devotional

There's no better way to start your day than to let God remind you of His love and all-encompassing generosity and grace.

These devotions from Steve McVey will point you to the words of Scripture and remind you to leave behind performance- and fear-based Christianity. They'll help you grasp anew that God's grace is immensely more than a doctrine—it's how He operates the universe. And He's invited you to enjoy it with Him!

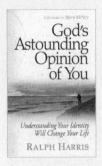

God's Astounding Opinion of You
Understanding Your Identity Will Change Your Life
Ralph Harris

Do you know that God's view of you is much greater than your own? Ralph Harris, founder and president of LifeCourse Ministries, leads you to embrace the Scriptures' truth about what God thinks of you—that you are special to Him, blameless, pure, and lovable.

With clear and simple explanations and examples, this resource will help you turn toward the close friendship with God you were created for.

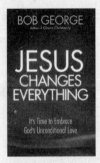

Jesus Changes Everything
It's Time to Embrace God's Unconditional Love
Bob George

Salvation is a free gift, but trying to live up to what you think God demands can feel like anything *but* a gift.

The problem? You're basing your Christianity in the Old Testament—making your faith a law-based religion. But the New Covenant, which God has put in place through Jesus' death, changes everything:

- effort, guilt, and fear from living under law give way to rest and peace from realizing your relationship with God doesn't depend on your performance

- motivation by punishment is replaced by inner motivation through His complete acceptance

- the sense of distance from God gives way to confidence in His unconditional love

Nothing could be better than experiencing the fullness of God's plan for you. This fullness is yours because Jesus changes everything.